Chernobyl Strawberries

VESNA GOLDSWORTHY left Yugoslavia in 1986 to marry
an Englishman she had met at the Karl Marx Institute
in Bulgaria two years earlier. Since arriving in England
she has worked in publishing and for the BBC World
Service. Her first book, *Inventing Ruritania*, a study of
the 'Wild East' of Europe in literature and film was
published to broad critical acclaim. She is currently
Senior Lecturer in English at Kingston University and
is Director of Kingston's Centre for Suburban Studies,
which she founded in 2004. She lives in West London
with her husband and young son.

'A lilting, lyrical and poetic musing on Vesna's comfortable childhood,
her marriage and move to Britain in the mid-1980s, cancer, and
what it was like to see her country disappear – bit by bloody bit...
a hauntingly honest account.' Eve-Ann Prentice, *The Times*

'Richly evocative.' Gillian Reynolds, *Daily Telegraph*

'Three qualities make Goldsworthy's memoir stand apart from ordinary
accounts: her honesty, her skill as a writer and the fascinating
circumstances of her life... She writes evocatively about the experience

of being caught between cultures, belonging to neither, and describes how illness finally allowed her to fuse the two different personalities between which she had felt divided, one speaking Serbo-Croat, the other English...*Chernobyl Strawberries* blows away the dust; Goldsworthy writes well, often beautifully...Memory provides her structure. Rather than writing chronologically, she leaps back and forth in time, following threads – love, music, family, war – that send her zigzagging across her life...Goldsworthy's ability to find unexpected subtle connections in the pattern of her own life elevates this absorbing memoir into something extraordinary.' Josh Lacey, *Guardian*

'Engrossing...She writes of her dual life as a Serb and an Englishwoman with refreshing candour...This is, in every sense, a reflective book, the work of a fiercely honest and cultivated intelligence...What is remarkable here is the combination of melancholy and absurdist humour...But this unusual book is chiefly concerned with survival and loss – the history that led inexorably to communism, and that of the frequently complacent West – and with lasting love.' Paul Bailey, *Sunday Times*

'Many good books are travel books in one sense or another, and this one charts a more complex journey than most...An exceptional memoir. If there has been a more honest, calm, and profoundly moving one written in the last few years, then I've missed it.' Andrew Taylor, *TLS*

'A charming book...Vesna Goldsworthy writes with wit and nostalgia about the vanished country in which she grew up...Beautifully written –

an elegy to a world that now seems so far distant that it is difficult to remember that it began to vanish just half a generation ago.'
Victor Sebestyen, *Spectator*

'Heavyweight and rewarding...Goldsworthy's treatment of her adopted homeland is masterly, using irony and self-deprecation to evoke affection, respect and clear-sighted criticism...She is equally sensitive but fair-minded as she considers her native Serbia, perpetrator of atrocities, but bombed by the country she now calls home...[The book is] a help to understanding the European continent's past woes and current muddles.' *The Economist*

'A profound and witty memoir.' Neal Ascherson, *Sunday Herald*

'Hers is a story that reaches inside you and leaves you with just a little more wisdom, a little less fear...Our own stereotypes of eastern Europe are cleverly excised in a book that is part a recounting of family life, part exploration of lineage and part quizzical portrait of a disappeared Europe.' Fiona Ness, *Sunday Business Post*

'A beautifully written memoir, you'll be left in no doubt about Vesna Goldsworthy's strong sense of herself, nor about her courage and her honesty... An uplifting but utterly unsentimental memoir of a life lived truthfully and without compromise.' Roslyn Dee, *Sunday Tribune*

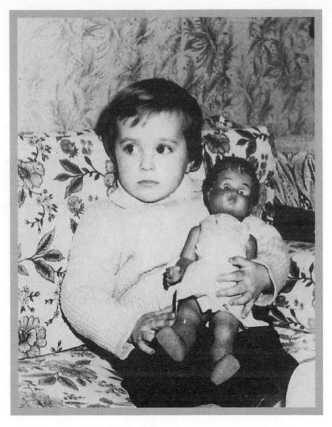

Two years old

Chernobyl Strawberries

A MEMOIR

Vesna Goldsworthy

Atlantic Books
London

For Alexander

First published in hardback in Great Britain in 2005
by Atlantic Books, an imprint of Grove Atlantic Ltd.

This paperback edition, with new endmatter,
first published by Atlantic Books in 2006.

9 8 7 6 5 4 3 2 1

A CIP catalogue record for this book is
available from the British Library.

1 84354 415 6

Printed in Great Britain by Clays Ltd, St Ives plc
Design by Lindsay Nash

Atlantic Books
An imprint of Grove Atlantic Ltd
Ormond House
26–27 Boswell Street
London WC1N 3JZ

CONTENTS

It is so difficult to find the beginning. Or better: it is difficult to begin at the beginning, and not to try to go further back.

Ludwig Wittgenstein, On Certainty

1

THE BEGINNINGS, ALL OF THEM

I have tasted Chernobyl strawberries. Every spring, winds from the Ukraine bring rain to the fruit nurseries in the hills south-west of Belgrade. In the city, the trees and cobblestones glisten. The scent of glowing berries – the colour of fresh wounds and as warm as live blood – spills through the streets around the market square. The fragrance lingers in the rusty tramcars winding their way around the old sugar factory and the promise of summer overpowers for a while the familiar smells of sweat, tobacco, machine oil and polished wood.

In 1986 – the year of Chernobyl and the spring before the summer of my move to England – their smell seemed headier than ever. I was twenty-four and in the kind of love that makes the oceans part. I was about to leave an entire world behind without a second thought in order to live that feeling to its end, wherever and whenever the end happened to be. There was no other option. I was, obviously, still a child: not because the move to the other end of the continent wasn't worth the effort (it was, it was!), but because I could, at that stage, think about love only in grand operatic terms. As far as affairs of the heart were concerned, when the *faites vos jeux* moment came I simply had to stake everything. Anything less and I might have lost my nerve.

The world I left behind, and which I am now revisiting from the distance of twenty years and well over a thousand miles, was that of Yugoslavia in the throes of the big communist experiment. As a social order it seemed invincible, yet it lasted just half a lifespan. Yugoslavia no longer exists, not even as a name, but in a kind of Rorschach test I still see the land of the South Slavs on every map of Europe. It is a vision which dates me: the way in which my eye still arranges its constituent parts into a country on the salty palm of the Balkans, the way in which I still call myself Yugoslav, and my mother tongue Serbo-Croat, without thinking, as though the very act of leaving, paradoxically, makes it impossible to let go.

The shape of Yugoslavia marks the outline of my childhood like a fat silkworm or a ripe white mulberry on the eastern edge of the Adriatic, but I am not given to homesickness or nostalgia.

I am English now; I wouldn't begin to know how to return to Serbia, which is not the place I left anyway, nor even to Belgrade, the only city in that corner of the world to which I have a link that still breathes. In that city, I enjoyed a prosperous childhood and adolescence in a sequence of more or less comfortable homes which became increasingly opulent as my parents' careers advanced and then poorer again as the country began to slide towards its final bloodbath. I rarely think of those homes and those streets nowadays. Nothing reminds me of them. Sometimes, nonetheless, the memory returns, uninvited.

———

Mine is in no way an exceptional story. I was an ordinary bright girl in an ordinary middle-class world with its own rules and regulations, communist comrades notwithstanding. I obeyed when I was supposed to obey and rebelled at all the right moments. On the surface, it would appear that there is little that is remarkable about my life story. It would be difficult to turn it into either *Speak, Memory* or *The Gulag Archipelago*. I was no Russian dissident: I have never seen the inside of a prison cell, never been tortured for any beliefs. I didn't escape to the West under a train or through barbed-wire fences. Much though I would have liked to, I've never had to memorize any poetry,

mine or anybody else's, in order to preserve it for future generations. The closest I ever came to a conflict with the communist
power machine is a heated argument with Yugoslav customs
officers over some LPs I was bringing back from Paris in 1980,
shortly after my nineteenth birthday. Two uniformed ruffians
threatened to make me get off a train in the middle of a Slovene
forest for trying to smuggle Western goods into the country. It
was an empty threat, the acting out of the rituals of an authori-
tarian state, a show of power and supplication aimed at putting
a spoilt metropolitan brat in her proper place. You don't stop
trains for Georges Brassens, not in Yugoslavia.

How could something that seemed so solid perish so easily?
I am almost disappointed that the comrades didn't put up a
better fight towards the end. I know they were tired, but they
owed that much to all those among us who had demonized
them so wholeheartedly. How could they just pack up and
retire to write memoirs full of dates and self-justifications? How
could they metamorphose so easily into a bunch of cuddly
grandpas with bad dental work? Even those who tortured and
imprisoned, and pinned electrodes to grown men's balls, now
wear checked slippers and send grandchildren to Western
universities. Their erstwhile victims, meanwhile, appear ever so
slightly mad and certainly much less nice, much less affable, less

well adjusted, as though they were, in some way, asking for it all along. Could it really be that I grew up in a world behind the looking glass, which had no more substance than the painted backdrop on a theatrical stage?

———

In the year of my birth, 1961, my extended family of six lived in two earth-floored rooms – mother, father, grandmother, grandfather, great-grandmother and the baby (me) – without an indoor lavatory and with a water tap by the garden gate. The poverty was both that of the country and ours alone. We kept being punished by circumstance, but also by a certain unwillingness to adapt, until we learned to adapt all too well, on autopilot, and to live without believing. Only then did the rewards begin to accrue. By the time I was twelve, we owned an enormous house, approximately four rooms and a bathroom per person (there were five of us by now: add another child and subtract the grandfather and the great-grandmother). We must have learned a lesson or two.

The New House stood, white and unmistakable, on the brow of a Belgrade hill, as a monument to my parents' drive and willingness to do without, surrounded by pine saplings which promised a mature garden for the grandchildren. It took five years to build and it was best loved in construction. I played hide-and-seek in the trenches dug out for the foundations and, when the walls went up, signed my name furtively in wet, salmon-pink plaster.

In the eighties, Yugoslavia – and most of us in it – went into economic decline. We could no longer afford to heat such a vast place and, even if we could, there was no oil to be bought anywhere in town and, because of power shortages, electricity on alternate days only. Our erstwhile buddies from the International Monetary Fund were beginning to tighten the screws on the comrades and they then turned on us, inventing more and more complicated ways of saving money to repay the foreign debt. Cars whose number plates ended in even numbers were not allowed to move on even dates, odd numbers on odd dates; Belgrade was divided into zones which had no electricity according to a complex rota announced every morning on local radio; sanitary towels were sold in particular chemist shops on particular days of the week, according to a schedule published in the daily newspaper; shops no longer gave out carrier bags, so you had to carry one in your pocket just in case you bought something; doctors' surgeries ran out of latex gloves, so you had to bring a pair if you wanted to be examined. Nothing major, nothing dreadful, nothing worth mentioning ever really happened, just a series of petty obstacles to remind us all that Yugoslavia was no longer the golden child of the West, no more the cutest of the Eastern babies. There were new kids to be cared for, grown lean and hungry on the Soviet diet, opening their pink little-baby mouths towards the teat, cooing just as sweetly.

I now realize that our housing and our family were never quite in sync and this seems to me the very essence of the East European condition. Built in the short-lived golden age of Yugoslav socialism, the New House represented an idea rather than an edifice of bricks and mortar. Like a mausoleum, it embodied – literally – my parents' dream of a large extended family, of generations multiplying and staying put, a Mediterranean hubris flying in the face of so much Balkan history and so much displacement. Whenever I think about this, it hurts. I've never even thought, not for a second, of fulfilling their longing for me to go forth – or, rather, to stay put – and multiply. I entertained the very Western idea that my first responsibility is towards my own happiness. I have been paying for this presumption with the small change of guilt every now and then. Of all the languages I know, guilt is the one that my memory speaks most fluently.

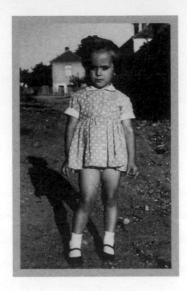

Three years old

Throughout the sixties and the seventies my mother headed the finance department of Belgrade's City Transport Company and my father was a code-breaker working for the General Staff of the Yugoslav National Army. My sister was, well, my younger sister. My parents' professions may sound quite grand, but they were an ordinary couple, the original yuppies of the sixties' boom, preoccupied with the upbringing of their two daughters and everything that implied – from French and piano lessons (yuppies, as I said) to summer holidays on the coast and winter holidays in the mountains. My family moved from being shepherds to skiers in three generations. This had nothing to do with the socialist transformation of the working classes and everything to do with my grandparents' ultimate realization that only that which is in our heads cannot be taken away. We were pushed so hard we'd have made the same leap on the moon.

My mother's job involved endless hours of overtime, when she was so immersed in bus-fare changes or the implications of zone alteration that she spoke of them all the time until even my grandmother and I began to discuss the issues involved with some authority. My father's work was so hush-hush that I had no idea what he actually did until I reached my late teens. He worked in a room full of cupboard-sized computers which, I now realize, had collectively less memory than an average PlayStation. In order to visit him in his office, one had to go through multiple security checks, passing solemn men in khaki uniforms along the vast corridors of a forbidding edifice which was bombed to smithereens by NATO back in 1999. My boys smashed Daddy's office. How much more can a father forgive?

Compared to the world of my grandparents, the four of whom managed to live and die in a number of different kingdoms and empires without properly leaving home, all the while acquiring unwanted expertise in the finer nuances of the differences between POW camps, labour camps, concentration and death camps, my own world seemed as dull and stable as something

9

out of a late-nineteenth-century bourgeois play. I went to school and did my homework, I read, I played, I collected pictures of film stars and basketball players. Vladimir Visotsky and Robert Redford were my favourites. I marginally preferred the Californian over the Muscovite, not entirely without reservations, which may or may not be telling. The Muscovite was suicidal, the Californian in love with himself.

Even as a ten-year-old, I was attracted to such contrasting extremes of masculinity that it was practically impossible to think of one Prince Charming who could unite all those aspirations into one. The quest for a self-destructive bad boy who would have a steady job, support the family and certainly never ever beat or cheat was soon on. I dressed up, I went out to dances and to concerts, I kept falling in and out of love. I grew my hair long, I cut my hair short. The world was barely moving. I was waiting for my life to begin. I believed in nothing very much, but – for reasons which I cannot now begin to fathom – I believed in the supreme power of romantic love. That, comrades, is the real opium of the masses: the belief that destiny and not you is uniquely responsible for our happiness; the obstinate belief that love will conquer all. It takes a lifetime to shake off. They peddle it in the West too; it is the most useful of distractions.

My family has lived in the Belgrade suburb of Zharkovo, at the end of the same tramline, for the best part of the last ninety years. A pretty village on the town's edge, it gradually grew into a grim socialist satellite town, a Legoland of ugly apartment blocks full of Serb refugees from Bosnia and Croatia. The only buildings of any beauty were old peasant houses, of which a few were left standing, an old Turkish inn which housed a forlorn cake shop, and one or two pre-war industrial edifices in the style of the European Modern Movement. With their shattered windows and rusty gates, they looked derelict and abandoned but for the fingers of sweet grey smoke pointing towards the changing skies from the tall chimneys.

My paternal grandmother once ran a beet farm which supplied raw material for the local sugar plant, whose building now houses an experimental theatre. Cart-loads of jolly cadavers, plump white bodies speckled with wet earth, made their way from our land in the flood plains of the Sava river, just before its confluence with the Danube, to the grim industrial courtyard dominated by the saw-edged roof line under which molasses boiled and brewed throughout the autumn months. My grandfather worked in a quarry which provided stone for houses and graves in this part of town. Both the homes and the graves were inhabited by recently urbanized, dispossessed peasants and – in small houses with deep verandas hidden by gardens and vine pergolas – the few professionals needed to look after them: the priest, the teacher, the doctor, the small-time solicitor (wills and property disputes).

In the cemetery on the edge of the village, now bisected by a four-lane motorway, my grandfather's name – Petar Bjelogrlic – was inscribed just to the right of centre on a black marble gravestone back in 1962, and left waiting until 1990 for my grandmother's to complete the celestial symmetry. Petar died at the age of sixty-eight. Fourteen years younger than him, my grandmother Zorka remained a widow for twenty-eight years. In its oval porcelain frame, my grandfather's photograph, taken soon after the Second World War, shows a melancholy, handsome middle-aged man with grey eyes and a blond mous-tache twirled at the ends. He looks like a reluctant dandy, uncomfortable in his stiff collar and thin black tie. Next to him, in a photograph from the seventies, my grandmother gazes straight to the camera with her coal-black eyes, white hair in a neat chignon, with the faintest of smiles on her lips. She is still wearing her widow's weeds and could almost be his mother. We are forever remembered at the age at which we die, but this particular funerary photographic mismatch makes it difficult to imagine what kind of husband and wife they might have been. I remember Zorka well; Petar, not at all.

He was a bright Serb boy from Herzegovina who was drafted against his will into the Austro-Hungarian army during the First World War. He wound up in Belgrade after the Armistice with hundreds of others in tattered uniforms, victors by virtue of their nationality, losers in their poverty and in every other way. He started off as a porter under the neo-Baroque arches of the central railway station and suffered horrible fits of homesickness, which he eased by seeking the company of his compatriots. There were dozens of young men just like him, newly arrived from the barren uplands of Herzegovina, in each working-class suburb of Belgrade. Born in the last decade of the nineteenth century as a subject of the Ottoman sultan, Grandpa died a citizen of the Socialist Republic of Yugoslavia. Between the crescent moon of Islam and the hammer and sickle of communism, his life changed little. He remained impoverished, hardened by long hours of physical labour, never fully at home.

He was in his late thirties by the time he felt ready to marry. His chosen bride, my paternal grandmother, was a Montenegrin, a fierce little wasp of the best stock that the southern

13

mountains had to offer. On her father's side, her people had been frontiersmen and warriors for generations, and, on her mother's, they were from the Nyegush clan, the ruling tribe of the theocratic Montenegro, providers of a succession of celibate prince-bishops who were Europe's ferocious alternative to the Dalai Lama. The genes of the mothers of all those tall, dark-haired and bearded Orthodox prelates with large silver crosses around their necks and princes with fur pelisses over silver rifle butts lurk in my genetic soup. For Zorka, Petar was clearly an act of rebellion and a half. *Plus ça change…*

My paternal grandparents' wedding (grandfather with full moustache, seated left)

Zorka's grandfather was given land around the city of Nikshich by Prince Nicholas of Montenegro as a reward for valour in the Turkish wars. Wounded in both legs on the battlefield and unable to move, Grandpa bit the throat of a Turkish soldier who was attempting to cut off his nose and stuff it in his trophy bag, and was duly mentioned in the Montenegrin equivalent of dispatches. Not to be outdone, his son received in his own turn acres of fertile black soil on the Hungarian border as a reward for a good fight in the First World War. In my grandmother's family, different estates are still remembered by the wars and wounds which brought them into our possession. The trophies came with a bloody string attached. Settlement on frontier land was always to be paid for with a pound of flesh.

Zorka moved closer to the centre of things when she accepted the offer of marriage and settled in our suburb of Belgrade amid the throes of the Great Depression. The young couple worked hard and bought parcels of land, and Franz Joseph and Napoleon ducats. The ducats proved the more solid investment. In the early forties, they were sewn into the hems of long over-coats and traded for food and *laissez-passers* as far north as the Baltic and as far east as the Ukraine. After the war, the fields were taken away by communists in exchange for a drawer full of impressive-looking nationalization certificates. I learned a thing or two about possessions from my family history. If you are ever offered a choice between ducats and land in the Balkans, take the ducats. In fact, generally, take the ducats and run.

All this happened after *this* war: that is how my grandmother used to refer to the Second World War. She died in 1990, talking about the imminent onset of *'war again'*. We never even tried to remember the difference between the many wars which seemed to divide ancestral lives into segments barely long enough to take a male child from his first nappies to his call-up. *This* war, which Granny also talked about as the 'German' war, brought the hated communists to power in 1945. Before it came the 'Austrian' War (*that* war, in 1914, in which we fought on both sides: Grandpa's lot for the ducat emperor of Kakania, Grandma's for the land-parcel kings of Serbia), and then one or two *Montenegrin* wars which coloured Granny's earliest memories of the world. Even longer ago – before she was born – there were the many *Turkish* wars of the 1800s, which put an end to 400-odd years of Stamboul khadis and pashas. They now populate the *sevdah* songs, the Balkan *fado*, the soul music my father sang so well, his fine voice thrilling to the mournful words we barely understood.

In the city of Istanbul, on the Bosphorus,
the pasha lies sick, dying,

his soul is breathing its last breaths,

his body longing for the black soil,

Allah, il'Allah, Selam Aleikum!

———

Any of these wars could have served as the beginning of my story. However, even though I come from a nation of inhabitants of history, supposed to dwell upon medieval conflicts as if they are still raging, I will desist and move on. For the moment at least. I was born on the first day of July 1961, although I don't remember any of it. I shared the day with Diana Spencer. Following one of my many career changes, I happened to be on the morning shift at the BBC World Service thirty-six years later to announce her death to Serbian listeners, who, in all likelihood, couldn't have cared less. Among the few who showed any concern was one of my cousins, who rang to say that my voice was inappropriately sad, for – after all – the princess died not like a mother of two grown sons but like a *midinette*, a Parisian sales-girl, in the embrace of an Egyptian millionaire under a bridge in the middle of the night. How undignified a death, he went on, how undignified! (Where I come from one is supposed to live each day as though it might just be one's last, not in any hedonistic sense but, rather, in trying to avoid – as far as one could –

being caught by death halfway through anything of which your family might be ashamed.) The death of Diana, therefore, was supposed to be a lesson for me. From a distance of more than a thousand miles, I was being watched over by a clan of dignified diers, and self-restraint was the least I could offer in exchange.

Among early death's role models, I also shared my birthday with Kalpana Chawla, the beautiful Indian astronaut who died in the Columbia shuttle disaster on the day I found out I had cancer, in February 2003. Numerical coincidences may well be poetry written by our autistic God: it is our duty to applaud. In fact, I feel a bit guilty about Kalpana, as though I had a small say in her death, for I walked back home from Charing Cross hospital half expecting, half wanting a greater disaster to obliterate mine, although nothing of the kind seemed to be happening. The boys from St Paul's School were rowing in a grey rain which was no more than mist, delivery vans made their way along Chiswick Mall, the sweet smell of yeast from Fuller's brewery filled the winter air. My husband was working, my son in his nursery, God on his throne somewhere above us all.

One of us had died six years ago, the second was dying with a bang, and the third was just beginning her (possibly) dignified long whimper. The differences might have been obvious from the start. Diana, Kalpana and Vesna, like Clotho, Lachesis and

Atropos, the three Fates, began their journey on the same day, under the stars that seemed to favour short-lived astronaut-princesses. But now only poor old Atropos, destined to live under the sign of Cancer and left to measure her days in strands of falling hair, remains to tell her tale.

———

On 1 July 1961, my Birthday Zero, Belgrade was blisteringly hot and my father was out on the Gypsy Island, where the voices of swimmers rose high above the river, and storks and fishermen shimmered in the haze of heat above the hazelnut-coloured water. My mother was polishing the windows of our little house when she felt the pain. No one had expected me for another month at least. I was a premature baby, weighing less than a loaf of bread. Nobody thought I would live beyond the first few months. I spent a couple of those in an incubator, while my relations consoled my mother by saying that she was a young woman, with enough time ahead to bear many more children, sons as well as daughters. She had taken a bus to the hospital, unaware that she was in labour. When my turn came, I walked from *our* little house to Queen Charlotte's Hospital in west London to give birth at four in the morning, watched by blinking street lights. Evidently, that's the kind of stock I come from.

What can this little cancer, this *tumourchich*, do to me now? Remember the Chernobyl strawberries? A pound of sugar for each pound of fruit and nothing else: that's the recipe.

The texture of warm strawberries mimics the texture of my tongue. The summer of my twenty-fifth birthday – my marriage, my journey to England, the early summer after the explosion at Chernobyl, of irradiated Welsh lamb and green lettuce – is just one possible beginning. There are so many stories one could tell. I am a bookish girl, a London university teacher, but I am also a great-granddaughter of shepherds from the Montenegrin and Herzegovinian limestone uplands, part of a cousinage of bishops and reluctant throat-biters. That's the kind of world we live in. My movement is neither more nor less unusual than any of my ancestors', at least not since they decided to leave the mountain ranges of the Balkans and get going.

———

There was Great-great-uncle Petko, literally Man Friday, who went off to Chicago at the beginning of the last century, returning to teach the children of antebellum Nikshich to shout 'Suck cock, son of a bitch!' without telling them what the words meant. My grandmother repeated the words faithfully seven decades later, although she suspected that she was saying something bad.

There was Great-grandfather Risto, Grandfather Christ – he of the Hungarian frontier fame. He worked in the mines of Butte, Montana, where apparently everything reminded him of Montenegro, until he finally returned, as a volunteer, to fight in the Great War. Montana and Montenegro became the mythical poles on our family globe. Throughout the long socialist afternoon, his grandchildren spoke wistfully of US passports which were allegedly all but ready when Christ volunteered to return. He never took his children back to the Land of the Free. We might have fought an entirely different set of wars.

There was Great-uncle Jovan, John the Gentle, known as Chicha, who became a sergeant in the *gendarmerie* in western Bosnia and married the daughter of an industrialist. When his town was overrun by the Croats in 1941, he escaped the death camps *en famille et sans un sou*, down the river to Belgrade.

There was my own grandfather Petar, Peter the Good, whose wars ended when he surrendered to the Russians in Galicia in 1916; there are defeats which are more honourable than any fighting. Petar, the lucky one, died in his own bed, the last rites and everything else performed, a dignified death.

There was even my maternal uncle Lyubisha, the Loved One, who spent a week in Paris hoping to become a tailor, then returned homesick to his village in the valley of the Morava.

The mournful farewells under the butter-coloured arches of the railway station in Belgrade lasted longer than his apprenticeship in the city of *lumière*. No sooner had we sent our first tear-stained letters than he reappeared on our doorstep. They are softies on my mother's side, the story goes, children of fat eastern Serbian soil, vineyards and plum orchards, *restaurateurs* and *podrumdziyas* or 'cave masters', who mark their years by the rhythms of wine making and not wars. They travel badly and wither when transplanted.

———

The novelty, this generation around, was that the women no longer stayed at home. They flew the nest, acquired incomprehensible degrees and sometimes wed foreign men, adding further unpronounceable names and new gene patterns to the monkey-puzzle that is our family tree. Unlike the men, once gone they tended not to look back. In addition to my own Anglo-Serb son, my wider family now boasts Franco-Serbs, children of a French-Swiss surgeon; Prussian-Serbs, fathered by a posh German banker; and even Hispanic-Serbs, the offspring of a casino owner from California.

My Goldsworthys are hardly outlandish. At least they were once our allies, my grandma said upon meeting a selection of tall, pink-skinned, blond-haired and blue-eyed future in-laws back in 1986. Above all they were neither Catholic nor Turk. And Montenegrins are just like the Pathans, my future father-in-law realized, looking at my grandmother in admiration, his size-twelve brogue tapping on our parquet floor, his tweed jacket too heavy for Belgrade in mid-May. Even without a shared language, they knew each other's type. While my grand mother smuggled guns from Belgrade to the hills, and lard back into town, under the noses of German soldiers, he spent *that war* in Razmak, in the North-West Frontier Province, an officer of the Guides Cavalry defending India from the Panzer divisions that never got that far. In Serbian, *razmak* means distance, so there was a shared language after all. It was a good marriage.

———

As it happens, I have my own war stories too. Before I got my first university job, I had worked as a small-time journalist. That was in the nineties, during the '*war again*'. Balkan expertise could easily be sold and apparently I had a Balkan story to tell. In the early autumn of 1999, I visited the northern Serbian plains to look at the molten toadstools of oil rigs hit by NATO bombs – dropped not more than a few weeks beforehand by my adopted compatriots against my compatriots by birth. The smell

23

of carcinogenic smoke and rotting animal flesh hung in the air. There was clearly a lesson to be learned there, but it wasn't about who had started the fight. The goodies and baddies were named in the nursery rhymes everybody sang; there was no point in adding my little foreign voice to the choir. In order to write I had to see. In order to see I had to go – over pontoons thrown across bombed bridges, driven by shadowy figures who had spent most of the decade charging foreigners the equivalent of my mother's annual salary for a ride around bomb craters and God knows what else. I learned how to deflect the 'where are you from?' question in my mother tongue. I lived a strange existence for a short while. I dined at the Hyatt Hotel with journalists in bulletproof vests getting drunk on expense accounts, with blonde rock-chicks and high-class prostitutes amid the sheen of marble lobbies where everything was for sale, while lodging in my parental home on the other side of town, where the windows were lit by the bright copper of autumnal trees and nothing could be bought. I could think of no questions to ask. I watched and wrote nothing.

I met a variety of politicians, opposition and government, in wood-panelled offices as big as football pitches, in opulent restaurants full of coke-heads and smuggled caviar, in lorry-driver *bifes* where they served tripe soup as hot as hell with cornbread and tiny chasers of homemade brandy, on park benches and in parked cars. I never sensed I was anywhere near the real story, whatever that might have been, and I hardly wanted to get there.

The Yugoslav Minister of Information, a tall and slightly rough-and-ready kind of guy, a former schoolteacher, invited me once to a white villa shaded by enormous chestnut trees in Dedinye, the Belgrade *quartier* where I lived between the ages of four and thirteen. We had a pointless conversation about the real nature of the conflict. In fact, I mainly translated the minister's rambling sentences to an important British journalist I was accompanying (the real reason behind a sudden flurry of invitations), while thinking about the cycle paths unknown to either of my interlocutors, who were both members of the male 'car and driver' International. They ran just behind the villa's walls right up to the hill above the military hospital, from which you can see half of Serbia on a clear day: its rolling hills, the shining ribbons of rivers, the flood plains, the plum orchards, the roofs of little churches like seashells amid lilac bushes.

The minister kept glancing over our shoulders towards a gigantic TV screen which showed muted footage of a basketball match. The villa was so eerily empty of furniture, it could have been the set for the third act of *The Cherry Orchard*. Both the party and the auction might have been in full swing, but we could see nothing from where we were sitting. 'God, Vezzna, what a colossal waste of time,' the journalist said as we caught a taxi back to the hotel, 'what a bloody colossal waste of time.' His sense of time-wasting was clearly different from mine, but I liked his wrinkled, intelligent face, with its mixture of gravitas and self-importance, a combination I couldn't muster in a million years. It worked well in my native city. So did the neckties and the inability to speak Serbian, neither of which could I sport convincingly.

In fact, I allowed myself to be exploited for such meaningless little interpreting sessions because I enjoyed the inconspicuousness they granted me. I passed on words like tennis balls and examined hands, shoes, paintings, views from open windows, men being cagey with each other in a series of ornate salons while women brought in coffee cups on little silver trays. Some of the women shot curious sideways glances towards me, but most of the time I could walk through walls unnoticed. I was four months pregnant and knew none of this would last anyway. The entire city smelled of rubble and recent fires. We drove past the bombed-out hospital through the leafy streets towards the river, where we joined streams of traffic on the main road. The buses were so full that they tilted heavily on every bend. I saw the suffering faces of old men and women pressed against the windowpanes and thought of my mother and my father in their cold rooms, on these buses, in long hospital queues. I desperately wanted to escape the bombed city and at the same time longed to stay on for ever. The *war again* was over and there was no excuse for hanging on as far as work was concerned. The stories were allegedly elsewhere. At the Writers' Club, the garden restaurant had already closed for the season, and Belgrade was gradually withdrawing into its smoky cellars and dives for the winter, the city willing itself to be invisible again.

———

Over the past couple of years, my body has been caught in a hormonal storm which wreaked havoc with all my operating systems. As a forerunner to cancer, I developed a disease of the eye muscle resulting in double vision, binocular diplopia, where each eye sees a single picture but with both eyes open one always sees two, partly overlapping images. It is a strangely appropriate condition which I found almost comfortingly close to my inner ways of seeing. For some eighteen months I could read only with one eye closed. Then the illness suddenly lifted. My eyes settled back into their sockets and started to coordinate again.

27

Immersed in theorizing about double vision, mainly in order to convince myself that I wasn't insane, I failed to notice the cancer (*my* cancer!) until the *tumourchich* became a proper, grown-up tumour, and was so large that it changed the shape of my breast. The healthy one lay flat on my chest like a milky pancake, the diseased one a beautiful glowing white mound straight out of a Renaissance painting, with a chocolate nipple which could have belonged to a fourteen-year-old. I now have a long duelling scar, like a smile, running diagonally across my right breast. On the scale of human misery, even within my own family, this barely registers at all. The doctors say it was simply bad luck – the illnesses could in no way have been connected. To me it seems that, for reasons which I can't bear to think about just now, my body was simply giving up. But I am a lucky girl, all things considered.

Discussing one's breasts in public is highly improper, particularly in my part of the world. I certainly hope this book is never translated into Serbian. This is not the kind of writing I had in mind when I penned my Nobel acceptance speech in pidgin French, in emulation of the Yugoslav novelist Ivo Andric, who wrote sprawling historical sagas set in Ottoman Bosnia. Not that I had read any of them at that stage. I was only eight or nine, but I already had a fancy that matching anything that Ivo did would make my parents really proud of me. I practised the speech in front of the double *armoire* mirror, under the reflected light of my father's green anglepoise and my mother's bedside lamp, shaded in frilly duchess satin. The same ambition, the same desire to please, the same vanity, amazingly, is still at work. Remember me. Remember ME!

In the spring of 1986, I made strawberry jam for the first time. I stirred the fruit carefully to avoid bruising. I dried rows of glistening jars in the oven. I filled them with sweet-smelling thick liquid. I wrote and dated the labels, adding short *pensées* on love and waiting to each, all in an effort to make time pass more quickly. Warm strawberry juice melting into the mountain of sugar made me think of the opening scenes of Snow White. Mirror, mirror, on the wall, who's the sweetest of them all? The princess of the Balkan kitchen might have been foolish but was no sacrificial virgin. I did not bring a single jar of my Chernobyl jam to England. I left them all in Belgrade, glowing on the shelves in neat rows. Or did I? The strawberries may or may not have been radioactive.

2

THE NAME OF THE MOTHER

Back in the eighties, still a young bride, I called myself Vesna Bjelogrlic-Goldsworthy. On paper, the name seems longer than its nine syllables. The grand double-barrel was a compromise between patriotism, the knee-jerk feminism of a Belgrade princess and that romantic-submissive impulse which leads women like me – two-thirds Simone de Beauvoir, one-third Tammy Wynette – to promise to obey till death do us part. Spelling the name out, however, soon became a bore. My fellow Serbs, not even willing to contemplate Goldsworthy, preferred Goldsvorti, Golsforti, Golzuordi and even Golsvorti, by association with the novelist John Galsworthy, whose high literary status in Serbia is reflected in the fact that he has his own street in north Belgrade. Most of the time, I did not bother to correct anyone over there, just as I've never put to rights anyone over here who expressed surprise that 'Vanessa' was a Serbian name. More appealing than Vesta or Vespa, Vanessa suited me well. It was my onomastic equivalent of an invisible cloak.

Bjelogrlic, pronounced Byelogerlitch, turned into an obstacle race for the native English speaker. It was indeed a fine Slav 'itch', as Evelyn Waugh once said, and anyone called *Ivlin Vo* must have known a thing or two about itchy names. Byelogerlitch means 'son of white throat', which, admittedly, sounds somewhat Sioux-chieftainish in English but is quite OK, even a *soupçon* distinguished, in Serbian. On my wedding day in November 1986, the registrar in Hammersmith took a deep breath every time he approached it and, remarkably, succeeded not once. I felt sorry for the poor man. The bride, the groom and the two witnesses (our entire wedding party) took a collective gulp of air every time he reached the B. What a job!

Since then, a rare few have been brave enough to try. Blog-litch was as close as one normally got. I dropped it after a while. I felt I had nothing to prove by endlessly repeating the tedious sequence – b-for-beetroot, j-for-jam, c-for-ecdysis, l-for-Levant, o-for-oh dear – and the variants thereof. I had too many names to care about any one. Even Goldsworthy is more than one should normally need to burden people with.

Occasionally, however – today, for example – I still feel a sudden impulse to teach the world and his aunt to pronounce Bjelogrlic properly.

———

The first Bjelogrlic was really, or *allegedly really*, a son of a 'white throat'. That belongs to the matriarchal story of my patriarchs. Early in the nineteenth century, escaping from a forgotten Montenegrin blood feud, my ancestral mother crossed the border into Ottoman Herzegovina with two young sons, unwilling to reveal her name to anyone. She settled in Lipnik, a mountain village no more than a stone's throw from her ancestral lands, but with a tribal frontier between her and whatever dispute threatened her sons' lives. The young widow's Montenegrin dress revealed more of her neck than those of her Herzegovinian Orthodox sisters, whose costume was barely different from the head-to-toe coverings of Muslim women. The colour of choice for clothing was black: ideal for both mourning and camouflage. It wasn't a world in which beauty brought anything but trouble.

Lipnik lay in the lands ruled by Smail-Aga Chengich, a feudal lord notorious for bloodthirstiness and the subject of a nineteenth-century Croatian epic in which my ancestors, now prime

32

specimens of the Christian *rayah*, the subjects of the glorious Turkish empire, were soon to feature with outstretched hands, begging, 'Bread, master, bread', before joining in the heroic uprising in which Smail-Aga (pronounced, sweetly, Smile-Aga) ended up brutally murdered, which was probably no more and barely less than he deserved.

—

The account of Smail-Aga's beheading, coincidentally at the hands of my Montenegrin granny's fellow tribesmen, remained one of her favourite bedtime stories. Over the years, like some Christian Orthodox Scheherazade, Granny had developed two highly picaresque versions of the same plot. One was a big battlefield scene in which a turbaned head flew with a swing of a Montenegrin sword, like a cricket ball hit by a bat. The other was an altogether more luscious but less probable version in which Smail is lured away from his troops by dancing Montenegrin maidens with promises of music and sweetmeats. The ending is the same.

The 'Turk's' head was taken to the Montenegrin court at Cetinje as a present to the Prince-Bishop and mounted on a contraption which made it bow to the ruler every time the door opened. If his subjects were anything like Granny, the Prince, who was a poet and a monk, would hardly have dared to complain about their gift.

'Mama,' pleaded Mother, 'this is not a story for children. They will never be able to get to asleep.' Her attempts to shield her daughters from such distinctly non-bourgeois versions of Balkan history were never an undivided success.

———

Many years later, Mother was again terribly upset when she overheard Granny telling my English husband how to preserve a human head. Their discussion, in which I acted as interpreter, focused on the relative advantages of pickling versus salting, a fresh take on recording Granny's favourite recipe. Needless to say, Granny had no experience of headhunting, but she sensed what my husband, a recent English graduate in Balkan history, wanted to hear, and she also thought that a hint of menace might keep her exotic grandson-in-law on his toes.

She delivered her opinions with a girly twinkle in her eye, and a wide, beheading movement of her wrinkled hand, while bragging about the fact that her ferocious tribe had achieved the ultimate accolade of being called 'whore's bastards' by their Turkish enemies. For a woman who had settled in a graceful and elegant former Austro-Hungarian town when she was barely in her teens, she seemed to me to have kept an astonishingly vivid link with the nineteenth-century Ottoman Balkans, as though nothing that had happened in the whole of the twentieth century could quite measure up to the triumphal defeat of the sultan in which her own grandfather had played a small part.

My mother's family (my mother is the tallest child)

In preparation for the day when my hair starts to fall out from chemotherapy, I line up sepia photographs of my Herzegovinian great-grandmothers, the wives of the sons of the White Throat, and copy the ways they tied their scarves. I suddenly realize that behind the tortoiseshell frames of my spectacles, behind the reddish curls carefully layered by my Thai hairdresser, behind the smile, which none of them ever shows, I carry *their* face. The mirror and the photographs reflect each other in silent recognition and I take my place in a row of unsmiling mothers with strong chins, large brown eyes, high cheekbones and tall foreheads. The eyes have it all, however. Having known real sorrow, I finally seem to have learned to read them. Ours is not a smiling culture. My grandmother maintained to her dying day that it was unseemly for a woman to laugh in public and covered her mouth with her right hand whenever she did so, even with us at home. Hers was the most winning laughter anyone has heard.

———

I am not quite sure what happened to the White Throat and whether she existed at all. I dropped the beautiful, unpronounceable name, which was her bequest, soon after I got my first job in England. Unlike my ancestral matriarch and so many others in the part of the world I come from, I have never been a refugee. I am not an exile. Not quite an expatriate either: that term seems to be reserved for those coming from lands which are more fortunate than mine. A migrant, perhaps? That sounds too Mexican. An émigrée? Too Russian.

All these descriptions contain existential drama, cultural baggage which is highly inappropriate for someone who walked down the greenest lawn in Belgrade to the embassy of her adoptive country and, after a long but very polite interview with the consul, acquired a letter addressed to the 'Under-Secretary of State' – I had no idea who or what that was at the time – asking him (or her, or it) to grant me the right of abode in the kingdom of the lion and the unicorn. Everything about Britain seemed touched with angel dust at the time. I could sit through the most boring documentary about the miners' strike or a royal wedding in order to catch background glimpses of my new home. I loved the embassy building, I loved the old-fashioned picture of the Queen on her throne hanging in the vestibule, I loved pouring little clouds of milk into my cups of Russian tea. *Un nuage du lait*: that's what Britain was for me.

The letter from the British embassy, printed on heavy white paper adorned with an impressive watermark, was to be produced at the airport on arrival. I left with an invitation from the consul to drop in for a cup of tea when visiting my native city again: I must have left a fine impression. That's how it was back in the eighties. Or that, maybe, is how it was for me. I was used to taking my good luck for granted, so I never knew.

Only at Heathrow, briefly, did my story touch those of others.

The immigration officer decided that I needed to have my chest X-rayed and I was whisked off from Terminal 2 to a clinic in Terminal 3 in a minibus driven by a chatty woman in a grey and navy uniform. There were other people waiting to be seen – a worried Indian woman in a sari, an African family, a man in a strange green suit reading an Armenian book – but I was out before I could take a good look at any of them, my X-ray filed somewhere in the airport building, where, for all I know, it may still be. Only minutes later, I was on the Piccadilly Line – the Ellis Island of London's huddled masses – with a copy of the *London Review of Books*.

———

One and one eventually became three. I am now a mother of a little boy. I earn my living teaching at an underfunded university in a prosperous London suburb. Daughter of a self-managed workers' paradise, I excel at my job. I criticize and self-criticize, I censor and self-censor, I compose self-assessment sheets about self-managed time, I sit on teaching and research committees, I attend meetings and take notes, I know that literature has hidden and insidious meanings. I have even written a book about those. My communist upbringing, my upbringing in communism – to be able to live with myself without believing in anything I say, to be able to accept things without asking too many questions – has certainly stood me in good stead throughout my working life. A virtue is a virtue wherever you are, East or West. A transferable skill.

Housed in a cluster of seventies buildings, the university is more like a piece of the homeland I left behind than anything still remaining in it. Remove the student union shop, empty the car park, add a few tramlines below and a mesh of trolleybus wires above, and you could be back at Belgrade City Transport thirty years ago. Walking towards the lecture theatres on crisp mornings, when the Thames, hidden behind neat rows of Edwardian villas, smells of rot and clay, I sometimes feel I am becoming my mother. My pace shortens and accelerates, my arms no longer wave about, I tread as elegantly as I can in my cowboy boots, and when I sit down I keep my hands in my lap and my back upright. I say no thank you and yes please. I smile. My eyes are blue.

—

My mother's office is full of supplicants – members of her staff asking for a swap on the work rota or a day off for a spurious funeral, pensioners complaining about the slow issue of travel-cards, foreign students with vouchers gone astray. The room is full of cigarette smoke. (My mother doesn't smoke, but practically all of the men and quite a few of the women who work for City Transport are chain-smokers.) A picture on the wall shows Comrade Tito, the Yugoslav President, inside a brand-new trolleybus. He wears the grey uniform of a marshal of the Yugoslav National Army, with more buttons on it than on the dashboard he is leaning against. Below Tito's picture is a large street map of Belgrade, with a spider's web of bus routes in blue, trolleybus routes in green and tram routes in red. My mother knows each of these by heart. At home, we sometimes play a game which consists of asking her questions about imaginary itineraries – what is the best route, for example, from Patrice Lumumba Street in Karaburma to the International Brigades Avenue in New Belgrade, on the other side of town – and she reels off line numbers, interchanges and frequencies. It is a game my mother loves.

Her office houses two large desks with telephones and typewriters, a couple of heavy leather armchairs and a small table with a ficus plant and an overflowing ashtray. When a visitor comes, Mother telephones for small cups of bitter coffee from the canteen in the basement. Anyone important is announced by a security officer, a large woman called Stanka, who wears a black leather jacket and short boots which end just below her melon-like calves and look as though they were designed by NASA for Mars landings. Under her jacket, Stanka has a wide belt with a pistol in a fine leather holster. She is a gregarious woman. She often laughs loudly and her belly moves up and down. Her pockets are full of boiled sweets, which she hands out to my sister and me when we visit.

My mother never forgets to ask Stanka about the health of her only child, Stanko, a little boy whose legs are thin and spindly, like cooked spaghetti. The security officer is the only single mother we know in the whole of Belgrade, and we feel sorry for her little son, as though he were an orphan, or worse. We cannot begin to imagine what his sad, fatherless life must be like. Stanka often repeats that Stanko is the only man in the entire world she would cook and wash for. 'Men, they are all the same,' she laughs, and puts her big hand over the pistol holster. 'They all deserve to rot in hell.' My mother doesn't laugh. 'Off to work, woman. Off to work,' she says, and gives Stanka a pat on the back with her small hand, a large amethyst and gold ring glinting against the heavy leather jacket. Stanka seems almost a foot taller than my mother.

There are three telephones on my mother's desk. They ring all the time and she often speaks on two lines simultaneously. My mother's secretary, a middle-aged white-haired man called

Toma, without the index finger on his right hand (a hunting accident), comes in and out of the room carrying bits of paper for my mother to sign. (I can't remember whether the absence of a digit affected Toma's touch-typing speed.) Many of the supplicants assume that Toma is the boss – communism notwithstanding, Yugoslavia is still a patriarchal place – and start repeating their stories of misfortune when he enters. When Toma points out the error of their ways, they return to my mother with a syrupy flow of apologies.

I sit in one of the armchairs with a glass of raspberry squash and listen, waiting for my mother to finish work. She keeps telling everyone about my exceptional school results and the supplicants smile at me ingratiatingly. I am embarrassed, proud and pleased at the same time. I tell everyone I want to be a poetess when I grow up.

It is 8 March, International Women's Day. Most of the visitors and quite a few employees bring in a bunch of flowers or a box of chocolates. My mother's desk is covered with cards, some of them with the picture of Klara Zetkin, the German communist leader, whose square jaw reminds me of Stanka. By the end of the afternoon, the hyacinths almost overpower the smell of smoke. I am here to help Mother carry the presents into the car: it is one of my annual treats. For days and even weeks after

8 March we visit relations and friends, distributing the boxes of chocolates and potted hyacinths Mother got.

My father waits in our white Skoda outside. During the drive home, as always at the end of the working day, my mother runs through events from the office in detail, but Father switches off after a minute or two. You can tell when he is not listening any more from the automatic intervals between his yeses, but she carries on regardless. It is the telling rather than his responses that seems to matter to her. My sister and I know all of the many dramatis personae of Mother's office life by name, ethnic origin and family situation. We know their illnesses, their children's misadventures at school, the location of their summer houses and allotments, details of their spouses' jobs. My father never talks about his work. If you ask him what he does at the office, he normally says that he sharpens pencils or some such lark.

Mother leaves home at five ten every morning in order to be at work at six thirty. The ticket kiosks throughout Belgrade open at seven o'clock and she has a whole series of telephone calls to make beforehand. At seven, she telephones home to wake up my sister and me for school. She tells us what she's put out for breakfast on the kitchen table and which clothes she's hung on

43

the towel rail, and sometimes asks, 'What's new?' absent-mindedly, as though anything much could have happened in the two hours of sleep we've had since she left. At other times she says, '*Molim*' – 'Yes please' – as though we'd rung her. When we play office, my sister and I emulate this particular tone on imaginary air telephones. In fact, we often play office, and my mother brings empty form books, paper clips and pieces of used indigo paper so that we can issue forms in triplicate. We even have our special office names for the game. My sister – who is normally my secretary – calls herself Clementine. I chide her about sloppy form-filling, and she bangs her imaginary carriage return in noisy protest.

My parents, before me

Most people in our street go to work an hour later than my mother. Often, when I leave for school, I see her small footprints like rows of hurried exclamation marks in untouched snow. I know that she was the first person in the entire street to leave her warm house in the morning, to take her seat on an empty bus whose wheels churn the icy slush in semi-darkness. At eleven, I am already taller than her, with longer, wider feet. I feel strangely protective towards Mother's traces: their edges soften and blur as the day progresses.

My favourite time of day is the early afternoon, when we are back from school and my parents are not yet home. My sister and I riffle through the mail, telephone friends, cut pictures out of magazines and play music very, very loudly. We are latchkey children of sorts. My paternal grandmother lives on the floor below (our New House is three storeys high), but she is at work on her land most days between late February and late October. She tends to return at dusk with bags of fresh vegetables. We still own half a dozen acres of land in the Makish valley, most of it under maize, and my grandmother keeps an acre or so for tomatoes, peas, beans, lettuce and radishes. My sister and I love the smallest of new potatoes, which are barely bigger than pearls. Granny's vegetable patch is reached through a narrow path in fields of corn, with long dark sabres of leaves which make the wind sound like a distant waterfall.

My mother comes back from work at four o'clock, with bags of ingredients for supper, breakfast and the next day's lunch. She prepares the evening meal and the next day's lunch at the same time every evening. Between five and seven, the kitchen is a noisy, steamy cauldron of activity; this is the best time to hide away in one's room pretending to be doing urgent homework, while in fact writing poetry or simply staring out of the window, daydreaming.

My younger sister and I

My father also returns around four with a briefcase and a newspaper, and often with warm loaves of bread under his arm. He and my mother sometimes catch up with each other on the short walk from the bus stop. She travels home by public transport and he in special army buses which pick him up from the same street corner every morning and drop him off every afternoon, like khaki school buses for grey-haired boys. The schoolboy impression is reinforced by the fact that Father often carries his gym bag in his briefcase. He regularly puts in an hour's swimming or a game of five-a-side football at the end of his working day.

Between four and five he usually has his siesta. He summons my sister or myself to tell him about our day at school. Our stories, he claims, lull him more easily to sleep. At five, he wakes up and promptly disappears downstairs, to the manly equivalent of the kitchen cauldron – things which involve neat kits of screwdrivers, pots of paint and polish, the car with its bonnet open, like the shoe-house of the fairy tale.

Early on, I begin to think that I should have been born a boy. I can't break an egg without making a mess of it, while I am usually exceedingly quick at grasping the interior mechanisms of every domestic appliance and the precise order of the bulbs behind the TV screen. A sole man in a household of four women, my father welcomes my interest, though the guilt associated with joining him rather than my mother in the kitchen most frequently keeps me in my room, writing.

———

The army bus is full of handsome, jovial men in fine uniforms. When it stops on the corner, its doors often release a stream of laughter, through which my father walks towards us. It is quite unlike the long snake of the city bus, full to bursting with angry people holding tight twenty or thirty to each pole. My mother parts the crowd with sweet apologies, like Moses crossing the Red Sea.

From ten minutes to four onwards, my sister and I keep watch for their return, looking up and down the road like spectators at a tennis match. When we notice the small silhouettes of Mother and Grandmother at the opposite ends of the street, we run to help carry their loads: a mattock and bags of vegetables for Grandmother, who comes from the bottom of the hill; carrier bags for Mother, who comes from the bus station at the top. If my father is the first to emerge, we simply jump on him, clinging like limpets to each arm, and let him carry us into the house. This ritual is repeated until some point just before my twelfth birthday, when my mother takes me aside and tells me that such unladylike actions no longer befit me. After that, only my sister jumps, hanging off my father's right arm like a baby monkey, for two more years. I walk beside them.

The women in my family are tiny – my mother five foot two, my grandmother barely five foot. Returning from work, they sometimes round the corner at the same time: Mother click-clacking in her high heels, Grandmother slowly dragging her lame foot in the thick woollen socks and flat rubber shoes she wears in the field. Both women take enormous pride in their appearance: the younger in looking as elegant as possible in her tailored suits, the older in appearing as impoverished as possible in her widow's black, with a black pinafore apron and a black scarf. When she takes her scarf off, Grandmother's face is divided into spheres of dark and pale skin, like a diagram of the crescent moon.

If a neighbour stops to greet her, usually saying something along the lines of 'Why are you working so hard at your age? Why don't you take a rest and let the children look after you?' Granny sighs and responds, 'How can I? There is an entire family to feed.' Mother gets quite upset if she hears this. Supporting your elders is a matter of pride and yet – like that aunt of Proust's who would never own up to nodding off – my grandmother is absolutely unwilling to admit to being supported.

49

———

Even when they are not carrying anything, we run towards them, trailed by the barking from the neighbourhood dogs, who run along the length of each garden as we pass, in a doggy relay race. Grandmother greets us with a line of criticisms and complaints ('You take so long, you lazy children. I'm so tired. I'm so thirsty. Why do I have to work for you?'), my mother with a hug and a smile, but we know that they are equally pleased to see us. Once Mother's back, the Arcadian atmosphere of our day is replaced by mayhem for three or four hours. She prepares our meals, dusts and cleans and washes, makes things for the deep-freeze and things for the larder, and compiles the ledgers of household bills. When all of this is done, she watches television, reads or knits. Rarely but quite regularly, she disappears to cry in the darkness of one of the bedrooms. She does so noiselessly, without sobbing. You wouldn't know that she was crying unless you asked. We don't ask. We know that if we did she'd cry even more. After a while she washes her face and comes back to us.

———

When she was eighteen, my mother came to Belgrade from a village in eastern Serbia to study French and Arabic at the university. Her father wanted her to become a journalist and, when he picked her up from the train station in his horse-drawn carriage, they often spoke of the distant places she was going to report from one day. Mother was from a wealthy restaurateur's family which once had lots of land and several houses arranged around a shady central courtyard full of dahlias and sweet peas. They had plum, apple, and peach and apricot orchards; a large vineyard on one of the best slopes in the village; a pepper and aubergine nursery dissected by a grid of small canals with streams of clean water; and a *bostan* – a field set aside for orange, green and yellow melons, and huge emerald balloons of watermelons on a necklace of leaves trailing on dry, fragrant soil. Mother told me how sometimes, in the evening, they used to throw the largest watermelons into the lake at the bottom of the field, and let them cool through the night, bobbing on the translucent surface of the water. They were ready to be picked up during the following morning's swim.

After a year in Belgrade, Mother had to return home to eastern Serbia. Her father and grandfather were both in prison for failing to deliver an impossible quota of grain to the state. At the same time, land was being taken away in order to create large state farms in the process known as collectivization, through which the peasants became state employees. My grandfather was ill-suited to becoming anyone's employee. He had already been jailed in the Second World War and was now on a big-time collision course with the socialist state. My earliest memory of him is of hearing the vilest of curses directed at the TV screen on which President Tito walked proudly, arm in arm with some African leader whose people's liberation struggle my country was generously supporting.

Grandfather returned from prison with raging tuberculosis and something that my mother always referred to as 'open caverns', bleeding wounds inside his chest. Paradoxically, by the time he was released the government's policy had changed and the plan to put all land under state control was abandoned, but the family was never the same. Their restaurant was requisitioned as warehouse space and the land – with low purchase prices and high delivery quotas enforced by the state – was insufficient to keep the family going. Their horses were sold off, their coaches rotted away in empty barns. They were hungry amid some of the most fertile fields in Europe.

I remember childhood visits to my maternal home, when I roller-skated through the vast dining hall. The derelict kitchens still smelled of smoked meat, the ice house echoed emptily. I made complicated figures around ornate pillars and through swinging doors, bathed in the jelly-bean spectrum of light which came through tall glass panels inscribed with my mother's maiden name.

By the time she returned to Belgrade to continue her studies, she had switched to law, a subject she never much liked. She had to support herself and law promised a securer future. She got a job as a night-shift duty clerk with City Transport and stayed there for forty years. You used to, apparently, in those days: stay in the same job, in the same town, in the same country, with the same man, your entire adult life. You had to choose very carefully, and make your choices before you were twenty-five, after which the options narrowed dramatically. The dream of bylines from foreign shores was passed on to me.

My mother's father

During those summers I spent in my mother's village, I grew easily bored with the open fields and the relentless sun. I hid with a book in a guest room full of dark furniture and fading photographs of long-forgotten weddings and christenings. I remembered the room being used only once, when I was seven. The family gathered around the open coffin in which my maternal grandmother lay, aged fifty-two, her arms carefully folded across her chest. A few weeks before she died, she had taken me to one side and asked me not to cry at her funeral but to sing instead. I respected her wish. Although it felt unbearably sad, sadder even than crying, I sat in the corner of the big room, quietly singing a nursery rhyme, until Mother ordered me to stop. She had never ordered me to do anything before, which is one of the many reasons I remember the day so vividly. The table on which Granny's body rested in a luminous circle of candles was now laden with fragrant yellow quinces.

I searched through my maternal grandmother's vast dowry chests, looking for God knows what amid the layers of starched linen with fading embroidery. At the bottom of one drawer, under the lining of greaseproof paper, I found my mother's French exercise book. I leafed through pages and pages of neatly copied, carefully accented text. *'Je suis heureuse. Tu es heureux,'* said the last line, dated December 1949. The exercise in grammar suddenly seemed very personal. I returned the notebook to its resting place. I wanted to know whether Mother was really happy when she wrote this, but there was no way of telling.

———

In preparation for her wedding day, my maternal grandmother had embroidered countless pillow covers and hand-cloths with elaborate initials copied from some pattern book, but she had never learned to read or write. Although she was the eldest daughter of a wealthy family, she grew up in a patriarchal world in which education, even in its most basic form, was seldom deemed necessary for girls. In her turn, however, this illiterate woman became immeasurably proud of her own daughter's schooling. It was possible that she had kept Mother's French notebook as a treasured memento of some kind, although she would not have been able to read her own daughter's words; just as my own mother – in spite of all her education – will not be able to read this book.

———

You chose freedom, says my future father-in-law, who had obviously read too many novels by Solzhenitsyn. It appeals to him, the idea of this particular choice, even if it is not the one I made. Later on, when Yugoslavia descends into its bloody death throes, it begins to look like that. I've chosen freedom from the war, freedom to define myself along any lines I choose, freedom to like the British Army officers, with their posh accents, well-cut uniforms and thoughtful faces, who now make a career of running the Balkans on our behalf, even when I can hear detonations as background noise during my daily telephone calls to my parents and can guess who is playing with the buttons. God knows, my compatriots have done their share and I am certainly not judging anyone.

Ten years into my marriage and queues of my fellow Serbs and Montenegrins stretch in front of every embassy you can think of. My own walk across the lawn of the British embassy in General Zhdanov Street and the consul's invitation begin to seem unreal. Nonetheless, I am still, at heart, one of the spoilt generation, brought up on the dream of Nabokov, Kundera, Brodsky, Milosz, Kis, the Great East European Novelists and Poets (why do I remember only men just now?), writing the Great East European Novels and Poems. We were an endangered and protected species, the pre-1989-ers, equipped through the best education communism could offer and the unstinting love of our East European mothers to believe that the world owed us a living, arrogant from birth. Had the consul not invited me to tea, I might not have come here at all.

—·—

In June 1986, my husband-to-be brought me over to his large family home in Sussex to plan the beginning of our life together. We were both recent graduates and decided to cross Europe, from Belgrade to the Sussex coast, in the cheapest possible way, by taking a couple of bus journeys. The first long leg was to be on one of the twice-weekly buses which took South Slav guest workers and their families to Paris. Our rucksacks were lodged between buckets of pickles and white cheese, and carefully wrapped sides of prosciutto, the food of homesickness. Large bundles and string-tied suitcases offered evidence of the travellers' paradox: the poorer you are, the more you need to take with you.

My mother, my father and my sister drove us to the bus station in our white Skoda. It was a strange beginning to a voyage, a weird mixture of holiday and funeral. No one knew what to say. But go I must, and I went. We hugged for what seemed like hours, saying nothing, and I climbed on the bus in the full blast of some mournful southern tune. My parents and my sister stood outside and waved, silent, like creatures in an aquarium. My mother was the smallest of the three. I suddenly became aware that she was wearing one of my dresses, a frumpy floral print which only a few days beforehand I had thrown out as definitely unsuited to my new life in England. As the bus pulled away, she suddenly started running towards it, for no more than five or six yards, and stopped, frozen, just looking towards me.

———

In the long night through which I gave birth on the top floor of Queen Charlotte's Hospital, high above the terraces of west London, with epidurals coursing coldly through my spine, I switched from English to Serbian in the low moans I emitted between contractions. My Kenyan midwife, Esther, urged me on. 'Brave thing. Brave thing,' she kept repeating. 'It's almost over. It's almost done.' My son's crown was already emerging into the world. I shouted 'Mama,' as, I gather, sailors do when drowning in the open seas. She came to me, silent, wearing that dress.

3

MY OATHS OF ALLEGIANCE

One of my favourite uncles, Zhivoyin, was once a guards officer in the king's army and an important player in the coup of 27 March 1941, which brought down the Yugoslav regency and put an end to its attempts to appease Hitler. After a long internment in a German POW camp, my uncle returned to Belgrade and became some kind of big shot in the Yugoslav sports administration.

With his tailored suits, highly polished Oxford brogues and fine ankles in long black stockings, he stood out among the communist comrades in their strange costumes, vaguely related to some distant notion of a Western suit, and stranger shoes, cut like leatherette bricks. He resembled a bird of paradise in a poultry coop. Even his hand gestures, suggestive of great distinction, looked as though they might merit five years' imprisonment followed by thorough re-education.

In his memoirs, Uncle Zhivoyin described the daily routines of a guards officer with a remarkable lack of pomposity. We loved the moments leading to grand parades – from the tips for high-gloss boot and brass-button polishing to the ways of applying a thin layer of face powder. My macho Serb compatriots were outdone by their Romanian neighbours, who favoured a barely discernible layer of lipstick on officers' lips.

I'd never known anyone quite like my uncle Zhivoyin until I met my future father-in-law. The bearing, knowledge of shoe shine and brass, even some of the hand gestures: it was all there in this Old Etonian and Indian cavalry officer, but with a kind of dishevelled, devil-may-care dash which revealed the peculiarly British, old-fashioned and upper-class horror of anything that might be described as sissy, prissy or any other issy adjective.

I was sure that, in so far as any two people in our wider families would get on, my father-in-law and Uncle Zhivoyin would get on famously. My father-in-law, however, was having none of that. In the midst of some vigorous pruning in his Sussex garden, he declared that he couldn't possibly understand a man who pledged his officer's honour to the king and then worked for the communists. Not quite knowing how to respond, I suddenly grasped the sheer luxury of being a British male in the twentieth

century. Every conceivable counter-argument notwithstanding –
and I know there are many – the picnic rug on the moral high
ground still came in khaki and red, the colours of his beloved
regiment. My father-in-law stood on the high ground, wielding a
pair of secateurs, chopping, felling and dead-heading, without a
care in the world.

———

I swore allegiance three times, even without counting my
marriage vows, and I know a thing or two about both swearing
and allegiances. The most recent ceremony took place back in
1991. About to become a British citizen, I walked up to the office
of a local solicitor in Chiswick, in a room above an electrical
supplier's shop. A dark silhouette with fingers poised over a
keyboard was clearly visible through the frosted door panel on
which the partners' names were etched in copperplate Gothic.
The scene was reminiscent of the opening shots of a forties
detective mystery, except for the sound, which was that of click-
clicking rather than tap-tapping, and the no-smoking signs.

This was an important day for me and I was unusually
diffident. My knock on the door was barely audible. I needed a
commissioner for oaths to witness my signature on a document
in which I 'swore by Almighty God that I will be faithful and

bear true allegiance to Her Majesty Queen Elizabeth the Second Her Heirs and Successors according to law'. (That's it, then. No republicanism in this house.) In fact, I could have 'solemnly and sincerely affirmed' instead – the atheist option – but I preferred the poetry of the wording which invoked the Almighty. I had never made any pledges involving God before, and solemn affirmations were a bit socialist for my taste. This was not to be a trade union Labour Day picnic. Sadly, given the Miltonian frame of mind, I didn't even have to read the words out loud.

'Just sign on the dotted line, please,' said a small man wearing an orthopaedic shoe and a smile even shier than mine, as he stood up from the enormous desk which occupied a good half of his office. Everything in the room, including him, seemed to be mushroom-coloured and slightly mouldy, as though salvaged from a shipwreck. He shook my hand, I proffered a five-pound note and off went the form, in a pre-paid brown envelope, to the India Building in Liverpool, its name a solitary, faint echo of the kind of reading material which fired my childhood fantasy of Britain. I wasn't sure if Messrs Henty, Haggard, Kipling and Buchan would have entirely approved of a foreign woman, a 'sleeping dictionary', signing any document in her own hand, but at least I now knew that I could dead-pan as well as any of their heroes. (I still can't hear the words 'Her Majesty' without at the same time hearing a line of metallic bugles blowing heaven-wards. Luckily enough, in my circles at least, one doesn't hear them that often.)

My Yugoslav passport: first visits to England

My previous oath was given at a ceremony which took place in the dying days of February 1980, only a few months before my baccalaureate exams. These were called, appropriately, the *Matura* examination in Serbian, even if our maturity was not high on the list of aptitudes to be tested. The year ahead was full of initiation rites: my first heartbreak, my first holiday alone (in fact, with my sister, who, being a couple of years younger, enjoyed every hard-won freedom a couple of years ahead of me), my first autumn at university. This particular evening was to be the first of those firsts. With a small group of nervous fellow *maturants* gathered in the senior common room of my Belgrade *lycée*, each clutching a red carnation and a brand-new red membership card bearing a small black hammer and sickle, I swore allegiance to the Communist Party, which I was about to join. Not many of my former compatriots in that swathe of land between the nostril of the Adriatic Sea and the lush hips of the Balkan peninsula would now own up to having done the same (even if we all know who you are, my friends!).

In fact, the proper name of the organization I was joining was the League of Communists of the Socialist Federal Republic of Yugoslavia, but there was no poetry in that. The *jeunesse dorée* of Belgrade called it the 'Ka-Pe-Yot'. Its pre-war acronym sounded vaguely romantic, revolutionary and illegal, redolent of the heavy coats with astrakhan collars, thick silk stockings and night-pot hats of the twenties and thirties, and prisons in which you sat around a big table with the comrades, translating radical German philosophy and declaring that you recognized no court but the court of your own revolutionary party. If you missed the Spanish Civil War this was the next best thing.

Funnily enough, I don't remember the words of the oath, although I can pretty well guess what they may have been. I remember that I made no note of the event in my otherwise impeccably detailed diary for that year (the last year for which I kept a diary – sadly, just as the details were becoming more interesting, I seem to have run out of enthusiasm for recording them). It might be that I was aware even then of the need to airbrush the event, subconsciously mindful of its impending absurdity. I take it as read that the oath was not entirely in keeping with the one I subsequently pledged to Her Majesty (Ta-rraaa!), but the Almighty, probably even QE2 herself, will surely understand. Her subjects seem to me an increasingly fickle lot. Why I joined the Ka-Pe-Yot, and in 1980 of all times, is another matter altogether. Its head, Comrade Joseph Broz Tito, was already in a hospital in Slovenia, waiting for a leg amputation in readiness for all those grisly jokes about knuckle stews that were to fill the many days of his grotesque obsequies in May 1980, and even I could hear the water sloshing on the lower decks.

My father, my national defence teacher, and Tom Courtenay have a lot to answer for. My father was a reluctant communist himself (membership was part and parcel of his job description) and a strong advocate of a 'wait and see' policy in all things, but in matters political more than anything else. Where I come from, it is the option of the wise, yet I would 'wait and see' for no man. 'Wait and see' was my father's way of saying you might well regret this later. The more he reasoned, the less reasonable I became. I had to join and that was that. My mother didn't help. Not a member herself, even when her refusal to join the party was clearly detrimental to her career as a bureaucrat in public transport, she was nonetheless exceedingly proud whenever one of her daughters was chosen for something, whatever that something might be, and the comrades were no exception. They were still running the country after all. The careers she saw me in – Yugoslav ambassador to the UN, director-general of Belgrade TV, editor-in-chief of the *Politika* newspaper – all involved party membership. The fact that she did not wish me to join was clearly a bit awkward, but we never addressed that particular problem, just as we never spoke about the sheer logistics involved in chairing a session of the Security Council on the Hudson while making it home to Belgrade in time for dinner *en famille*, another thing that she would always expect of me. Such minor inconveniences would surely sort themselves out one way or another. As, indeed, they did.

66

If anyone, Tom Courtenay may have been the main culprit. In all those long afternoons of the seventies which I spent sitting in matinée screenings at the National Museum of Cinematography, in the roomy basement of a building in Kosovo Street in Belgrade, emerging bleary-eyed into the blinding light of the Balkan summer, few films affected me as deeply as *Dr Zhivago*. Granted, part of me knew even then that it was fundamentally a piece of sentimental trash, but the Great Russian Soul, as sieved through the quintessentially English melancholic view of history, was absolutely irresistible. The English played the Russians with the sort of respect and care that was only ever matched by Americans playing the English – one empire nodding to another in recognition that we are all heading in the same direction.

And *Dr Zhivago* was, for me, mainly about Strelnikov. Lara was an absolute blank, and the others were hardly worth bothering with. A wounded male in an armoured train cutting its way through Siberian snowdrifts (red flags a-flutter, gold-rimmed spectacles a-twinkling), embracing communism as a cure for a broken heart, Courtenay's Strelnikov was clearly irresistible. Like some blond angel of destruction hurtling towards his death because of that evil, corrupt Komarovsky, he was the man every silly fool in Belgrade (even if, quite possibly, nowhere else) wept for. There was no need to read Pasternak if you had David Lean, with all those comrades bleeding on virgin snow under the assaults of cruel tsarist Cossack cavalry, all the rich fur and rows of trembling birch trees, boots falling on the frozen surface of snow like silver spoons on *crème brûlée*, and all that lingering, annoying, sentimental music!

I knew even then that my communism was the stuff of Hollywood fantasy in which tall men and slim, bookish women argued passionately, and painstakingly printed illegal leaflets on small presses hidden in back rooms whose doors were as taut as the membrane of a drum, always about to burst under the policeman's heavy boot. There was no room in that fantasy for murderous stocky Josephs – Dzhugashvili the Georgian (a.k.a. Stalin) and Broz, the Slovene-Croat (a.k.a. Tito) – not even for the fatherly, dumpy Karl and Friedrich (Tweedledum and Tweedledee), let alone their ten (or was it eleven?) theses on Feuerbach we had to know by heart for our philosophy lessons. They were all clearly deviating from my party line. The philosophers have only interpreted the world in various ways, the point surely was to make it more beautiful.

Of course, you may say, Strelnikov/Courtenay had it easy, cast as he was against not only that Orientalist devil Komarovsky (Rod Steiger could hardly erase the memory of evil Jud Fry from *Oklahoma!* with his bourgeois little beard) but also the equally dark-haired, doe-eyed and totally uncool Dr Zhivago/Omar Sharif, who, his jauntily tilted fur hat notwithstanding, looked about as Russian as John Travolta. Wasn't that part of the plan? The West was clearly in love with its enemy, and I understood that love story perfectly well. It was underpinned by the same longing for simplicity, sharing and self-denial which now makes my British compatriots buy Shaker kitchens and wear Birkenstock sandals. Declutter, comrades, for heaven's sake!

———

My national defence teacher, Brka, the Moustache, a graduate in Marxist philosophy from a provincial university, was a handsome young man brimming with energy and wit. He obviously had the annual task of enlisting a select crop of eighteen-year-olds. Who could have been a more fitting candidate than the school egghead who simply had to excel in every subject, including his own? I can still tell you how to measure the distance between the sight of the gun and the moving target, according to the visibility of particular body features. I still know the butt of my M-48 from the muzzle. In fact, the year before I joined the party I practised with an airgun for a week in our back garden in order to achieve the best results in the school's annual shooting competition. Clouds of sparrows flew off our cherry trees with every shot, our dog leapt and barked, straight-backed and alert like an arrow by my right knee, in what was clearly some Jungian doggy memory of hunting (the only meat he ever saw came from the butcher's block or a tin). Blossom drifted aimlessly in the air. But for the din we were creating, we could have been in a Japanese postcard. Once I knew which eye to close when aligning the sights, I was away.

While congratulating me on my marksmanship on the bus returning from the shooting range, Brka added that he expected no less of me. During his national service in Bileca, in Herzegovina, he was once inspected on a parade by a kosher five-star Yugoslav National Army general by the name of Bjelogrlic. He was clearly under the impression that the man was my paternal uncle. He still remembered the general's grey hair, cut incredibly short and combed *en brosse*, the voice of calm authority with which he delivered a patriotic speech, and the missing index finger on his right hand. I have to admit that few things are potentially as manly as a finger blown off in the heat of battle. There are exceptions, such as my mother's secretary, Toma, but the loss of his digit is not quite the same thing.

I could hardly own up to the fact that I was not having tea with 'my uncle' the general every Thursday afternoon. In a sense we must have been related – as the White Throats all are, in one way or another, since there are no more than a couple of hundred of us extant around the world. As far as Brka was concerned, I clearly hailed from the right side of the tracks. That quite a few, even perhaps a majority of my wider family, might have been on the other side, or sides (in any war you cared to mention), was not to be looked at too closely.

Whoever was to blame or to credit, I was undeniably among the group of students gathered in the senior common room of our Belgrade *lycée* on a rainy February day, waiting to join the party which would barely survive for another five or six years. I am aware that the quaint French tag of *lycée* hardly does justice to the fifties, Mies van der Rohe-inspired, modernist powerhouse of learning and teenage romance I attended between the ages of fourteen and eighteen. 'Grammar school' sounds to me too earnest and plain, almost Quakerish, and 'gymnasium' too weird and Germanic for my alma mater, known locally as XIII Beogradska Gimnazija, and situated on the brow of one of the city's leafy hills. Today in Britain it would be called a city

71

academy. It educated some of the most intelligent and most fashion-conscious young people east of the Iron Curtain.

The city of Belgrade and its *lycées* could in fact be divided into three rings. In the inner ring – the *Centar* or the Town, as it was often metonymically referred to – the *lycées* were numbered in single Roman numerals, and were, as a rule, housed in neoclassical, butter- or soot-coloured edifices with roofs supported by muscular stone giants. These had been the boys' and girls' schools of the pre-war Serbian elite. The education system continued to be highly selective, perhaps even more so, under the communists. You could not get a place in a good *lycée* without a solid combination of the right kind of home address, high grades, parental connections and sometimes even expensive weeks of cramming for the entrance exam. (My sister, for example, inherited the same tutor who had put my father through his paces some thirty years before, an out-of-work pre-war university professor with a whole shelf of books to his name.) At least the schools were now free of charge and co-ed.

The students of the 'Town' *lycées* were a weird mixture of the sallow offspring of the newly privileged who occupied the grand apartments hastily abandoned by the old elite in 1941 or 1945, grumpy 'old Belgraders' of all persuasions who remained in basement and attic flats, and the bright sons and daughters of the new working class. The last group spoke a multitude of dialects and frequently sported improbable jumpers, knitted in their villages of origin using the wool of sheep with which they were personally acquainted. They lived four to a room in dilapidated tenements around the multitude of courtyards which clustered like honeycomb between the central boulevards. Their parents' names languished on the waiting lists for new apartments in the housing estates which were endlessly sprouting on the outer ring of the city.

The Corbusian vision of social paradise, which this replacement for the honeycomb embodied, looked like a beekeeper's nightmare. In it, settlements bore names of quaint old villages obliterated before an advancing army of cranes and scaffolding. There were as yet no *lycées*, only a few scattered and oversubscribed primary schools. Sleepy teenagers from the tower blocks arrived every morning via green city buses at the schools of the inner ring. The historic suburbs with wide tree-lined streets, where Art Deco apartment blocks on the main road hid fine houses with large gardens, were usually referred to as *brda* – the hills – and their gilded youth as *brdjani* – the hillbillies. The bus lines which brought the *peasants* – the inhabitants of the outer ring – into the demesne of the hillbillies of the inner ring bore the names of the old villages which marked their final destinations. Romantic names such as Cerak (Oak Grove), Bele Vode (White Waters), Visnyichka Banya (Sour Cherry Spa), Veliki Mokri Lug (the Great Wet Copse) and Mali Mokri Lug (the Little Wet Copse) obscured the drab socialist realities of what the Germans called *Trabantenstadten*, Trabant Towns. Bleak blocks of flats smelled of coal and sauerkraut. Amid them, children played on muddy lawns until summoned home by a piercing shout from a distant balcony. At dusk, parental cries multiplied, like the screeching of swallows or bats.

The in-comers from the outer circle normally formed little groups according to the bus routes on which they travelled. Hillbillies, meanwhile, were the offspring of Belgrade yuppies, who, like the children of New Labour in the Britain of the late nineties, preferred to forget where they came from and instead enjoyed the privileges of where they were at the moment. They dressed fashionably, read glossy foreign magazines available only by subscription, drove smart little cars imported from the West and enjoyed holidays abroad or in one or two select spots on the Adriatic coast. The walled old towns were *in*. Any resort with hotels belonging to the trade unions or offering package holidays for the *déclassés* from abroad was *out*. Any foreigner who could afford nothing better than a holiday on the Yugoslav coast was by definition to be looked down on. Membership of the Communist Party was itself clearly coded in the *Hillbilly Book of Etiquette*: as a rule of thumb, it was socially smarter not to join (and particularly smart to endure a meaningless job as a punishment for not joining). I was obviously committing a social *faux pas* of tectonic proportions, but then, owing to my family's somewhat eccentric movements, I was only a tentative hillbilly anyway. I was never entirely sure where I was supposed to belong, so I made a career of not belonging.

———

In February 1980, in our senior common room new members of the Communist Party represented a more raggle-taggle selection than before. Some were visibly keen, some rather diffident, some were obvious (clever-clogs, careerists with a bad sense of timing, those who carried a briefcase to school, prominent members of youth organizations, children of well-known communists who could hardly afford to refuse to join), some rather less so (ditzy girls from old families who had fallen for the hammer-'n'-sickle chic, the school poet, the fourth-grade hunk, a good third of the school basketball team, encouraged to join as role models and highly visible because they were all six foot six and chewing gum). Working out which members of the teaching staff belonged to the party, information you wouldn't

75

normally have been privy to as a student, was part of the privilege conferred by this particular entry into the adult world. The rest of the evening was a blur. An oath was said, a paper signed, the red carnation dropped into a litterbin on the way home. I still tend to avoid buying carnations whenever I can: they remind me of communists and winter funerals.

———

A year or two later my membership lapsed through non-payment of my monthly subscription fees. It wasn't that I couldn't afford the student rates, which were nominal; it was pretty obvious that the party was over, and not responding to the reminders for payment was the most elegant way of getting yourself expelled, if any expulsions ever officially took place, that is – I am not entirely sure. By the time of the first demonstrations of Albanian students in Prishtina in 1981, I had already ceased to pay attention to Ka-Pe-Yot and its sleazy eighties avatars. Long before the wall began to crumble in Berlin, Yugoslavs were busily denying any affiliation with their own Communist Party. You either tended to forget your membership entirely or put it about that you had been expelled, by the party secretary in person, for saying this or that straight to his or her face. There were usually no witnesses, and the secretaries were hardly likely to raise their heads above the parapet and put the record straight when they themselves were busily composing accounts of the dramatic events which surrounded their own expulsion.

The only people who still went around saying that communism was basically a good idea were the *Informbirovci*, the old communists who remained loyal to Russia at the time of Tito's split with Stalin in 1948 and did their time in the Goli Otok labour camp in the Adriatic as punishment. They were mostly senile and the only other thing they could remember was the Russian lyrics of the Internationale.

———

In fact, by the time I settled in England, I managed to forget that I had ever been a communist, and cheerfully supported the Conservative Party campaign in Hammersmith in west London, where I lived at that point, in its efforts to win the 1987 election. My great-grandfather-in-law was the first ever MP for Hammersmith (Conservative, *bien sûr*), although he was never poor enough actually to live in his constituency. Both a desire for symmetry and an East European allergy to anything that could be described as leftist, which is so often the first phase in our westward movement, can be claimed as mitigating circumstances. Hands-on experience of campaigning was an invaluable initiation into the rituals of Britishness. I was delivering leaflets, canvassing, urging old ladies not to forget to exercise their democratic right, counting 'our supporters' in a well-thumbed copy of the electoral roll. The prospective MP was a thoroughly nice chap. I was even introduced to his parents. Championing Maggie Thatcher, by now, probably seems like something that should be more difficult to own up to than being a fully paid-up commie, but what the hell? Comrades, I am your comrade again, I promise.

For at least a couple of years after 'we' won that election, I remained an ardent royalist and a true-blue Conservative, in what was neither the first nor the last of my spectacular political U-turns (by then, though, I was sufficiently aware of my own fickleness not to be inclined to formalize membership of any organization). It was disappointing to learn that one didn't necessarily become any wiser as one grew older, although the 'wait and see' policy – as advocated by my father – finally began to show distinct advantages. If you stood 'waiting and seeing' long enough, you were bound to catch me on my next revolution.

The Goldsworthy campaign trail

The only time I had to account for the communism business was before a bespectacled young man in the consular section of the US embassy in Grosvenor Square. In the eighties, before I acquired British citizenship, I had some entertaining times there applying for a US entry visa on my old Red passport. Obviously, I had to tick the Yes box against the 'Are you or were you ever a member of a Communist, Terrorist or similar organization?' question on the visa application. I needed to provide explanatory details on the dotted line and the best I could come up with was 'The Yugoslav Communist Party was never really a communist party and I never paid my membership fees.' Feeble, perhaps, but it seemed to impress the young man. In sheer bravado, I decided to tell him about my ongoing electioneering activities. The initial explanation was more than sufficient to get me into the United States, but I was not one to do anything by half. Before my very eyes, I was finally turning into one of those dissidents from Hollywood movies. I was the kind of woman who gamely sleeps with the hero on his brief assignment behind the Iron Curtain and is then sentenced to life imprisonment or casually shot at a checkpoint. The bespectacled young man played with the cuffs of his Brooks Brothers shirt. I loved his accent. I loved his college ring. I wanted to become his friend. Like Maggie, I was, at that stage, in love with everything American. I was eager to hit the road with my thirty-day Greyhound pass, counting on doing a state a day at least, with a copy of *On the Road* in my rucksack. A rejection would have been devastating.

My earliest oath of allegiance, way back in 1968, is the only one I still remember word for word, even after all these years. 'Today, as I become a pioneer, I promise that I will study and work industriously, respect my parents and my elders and be a sincere, trusted friend who keeps a given word,' I echoed in a choir of thin, seven-year-old voices, sixty or so kids from the first grade of the 22 December Primary School. We were gathered on the glorious stage of the central hall in the guards' barracks in the Belgrade suburb of Topchider, in front of dozens and dozens of men in uniform, teachers, parents and older pupils, all dressed up to the nines to celebrate our school day. It was also Army Day, hence the top brass: such attempts at across-the-line socializing were clearly good for army PR. The room was dripping with gold braid.

The new pioneers were dressed in identical white shirts, navy trousers and pleated skirts, white stockings, black lace-ups or patent-leather shoes, and brand-new triangular red scarves around the neck, with the emblem of the Pioneers' Union. The officers stood up and saluted with an outstretched hand, fingers aligned at an angle of forty-five degrees just above the right temple; the pioneers responded with a clenched fist, the longest way up, the shortest down. Fatherly figures looked down at all of us from the photographs suspended in large frames above the stage. In one of them Comrade Tito and his wife, Comrade Jovanka, were sharing a laugh with a group of young pioneers just like us. He was dressed in a white naval uniform, she in a demure little black dress with a posy of flowers in her hands, the beehive hairdo fashionable in the fifties towering over his officer's hat by a couple of inches.

Layers of fine snow, thick and softer than goose-down, covered the valley of Topchider, bedecking its former royal hunting lodge and sprinkling the hills around it. Snowflakes went on falling silently beyond the tall French windows, and their glorious light filtered through the white silk curtains. I stood out in front of the group and started reciting a long ballad about the glory and pain of the Fourth Partisan Offensive in 1943, when the heroic troops ('our fighters') marched for days from north-west Bosnia, across the Neretva river to the safety of Montenegro, with 4,000 wounded and thousands of refugees in tow. (A film version of the battle, with Yul Brynner, Orson Welles and Franco Nero, was one of those spectacles we later saw whenever no one could think of a better thing to do on a school away-day.)

My voice trembled as the presenter lowered the microphone by a foot or two, then steadied itself. I fluffed not once. My mother, resplendent in a sky-blue Chanel suit, with a little white fur collar and pearl earrings, her eyes filled with tears, led the applause from the fifth row. She was thirty-four, small and elegant, her eyes the colour of cornflowers, her hair the colour of mahogany, a glorious crown of thick curls. She was the most beautiful woman in that vast room. I was clearly the chosen one.

———

My sister and I spent the following day sledging on a hillock which was known to the local kids as Hiroshima. Halfway down, it had a bump which made the sledges jump and land about a foot further on, with the thuds of wood followed by thuds of little bottoms and excited screams. My sister, aged five, was a picky eater, weighing barely two and a half stone, with the long face of Anne Frank. She was endlessly pursued by my mother and my grandmother with spoonfuls of cod liver oil and tasty morsels of this or that. She subsisted mainly on crusty bread with homemade damson jam. We were known to take jars of jam on holiday with us for fear that she would not want to eat any hotel food, in spite of the protestations of my father, who argued that children never starved themselves to death if food was on offer, whatever it may be. On Hiroshima, my skinny sister flew higher and screamed louder than any of us.

I was just pulling her on a sledge back towards the house, our fingers and toes frozen solid and our lips and noses blue, when my father turned the corner, tall and imposing in his black Crombie coat, with a paisley scarf, black beret and black leather gloves. He looked like a fifties matinée idol, a cross between Cary Grant and Clark Gable, with a thicker moustache and larger, more sensitive eyes than either of those two. His face was beaming and he was carrying a small black valise with metal trimmings which looked like an old-fashioned explosive device. Once inside the house, he opened the valise to reveal a set of speakers and a turntable with a button which could be pointed towards 16, 33 and 45. It was the Beat Boy, our first ever, East German-made, gramophone. From under his long coat my father produced a vinyl record in a dark green sleeve. The faces of Julie Christie and Omar Sharif were staring at us from the cover, his puppy eyes dark brown, hers improbably green. In the corner of the room, below a tall Christmas tree which stood, still undecorated, on its wooden cross, I was being led into the foothills of my love affair with Strelnikov.

My father slowly took his coat off, carefully put the record on and asked Mother to dance. My sister went to fetch herself a *tartine* of bread and jam. The two of them, he large and tall and dark, she fair, tiny and childlike in her size-three flat fur slippers, just stood there looking at each other, and then at me looking at them.

My first LP

I last saw Strelnikov in early 1987, on the frozen platform of Budapest's Keleti Station, walking the twenty or so yards alongside my carriage, up and down and back again, little heaps of dirty snow crunching under his highly polished boots. His grey officer's overcoat and grey fur hat with a shiny enamel red star on it made him appear even taller than he already was. With his cropped blond hair and blue eyes he looked like a lost deity from some Slavonic *Götterdämmerung*.

My Belgrade-bound train was coming from Moscow and he had obviously been sent to meet someone who had failed to materialize. The station was dark and full of smoke and my carriage smelled of wurst and coal. People with yellowish skin, badly cut clothing and strange footwear, once so typical of winters in the Eastern Bloc, gave him a wide berth as they passed, their expressions filled with barely disguised hatred. He could not have been much older than twenty-five, a Russian boy who stood alone in an empty circle on a crowded platform, not looking at anyone, until, at one moment, he lifted his head towards the carriage and his eyes met with mine. I smiled. He gave me a long absent-minded glance, but his face remained inscrutable and distant. He never smiled back.

4

A POEM FOR COMRADE TITO

Between the ages of four and twenty-four I wrote poetry every day. It is debatable how far one could divide the days into good and bad as regards the production line, but on some I wrote as many as four hundred lines of verse – running up to ten separate poems – while on others I polished a single couplet until it had not a single word in common with the original version, and then back again.

I am not at all sure where all that poetry came from. Ours was a reasonably bookish house, but not a particularly poetic one. We possessed hardly any books of poetry. In fact, before I started buying books, our library consisted of my father's mathematics collection, mainly in Russian, and a haphazard assortment of nineteenth-century novels in an equally random selection of languages. Our entire book collection fitted into a single bookcase with fragile glass doors, locked by an ornate key with a wine-coloured silk tassel. A row of porcelain figurines which stood in front of cloth-bound editions of overviews of higher mathematics, *Kursi vishei matematiki*, published in Moscow and Leningrad in the late forties, suggested correctly that the books were seldom moved from their places, although that would be misleading as far as our reading habits were concerned. We all read like souls possessed, even if we did not own many books.

Books were very expensive, and if a neighbour or an aunt bought a copy of a novel – it might have been anything from the Croatian translation of D. H. Lawrence's *Lady Chatterley's Lover*, published when I was four, to Sholokhov's *And Quiet Flows the Don* in its original Russian – we all read it, irrespective of age and pedagogical advice. I was barely out of primary school when I asked an elderly great-aunt about how exactly – quoting D. H. Lawrence – one was meant to 'fuck a little flame into being'. *Lady Chatterley's Lover* was, in fact, my favourite novel before I discovered Saint-Exupéry's *Le Petit Prince*. That's how topsy-turvy my reading world was.

All of us knew a lot of poems by heart. Yugoslav *lycées* tended to make their students learn a couple every week. They adhered to strict learning programmes, which meant that the entire population of fourteen-year-olds up and down the country would be learning the same poem in the same week, and that my parents knew exactly what we were up to, because they learned exactly the same poem in exactly the same week when they were fourteen (except, of course, for those poets who have since disappeared from the face of the earth because they have said or done something not said or not done). We all agreed that the only poetry you truly possess and enjoy is that which you know by heart.

Both my parents retained an extensive selection of verse from the national Parnassus in their heads, even if they chose not to go around reciting it to their daughters, except on long car journeys when we ran out of songs to sing. My father had a preference for Sergei Esenin, and frequently recited an unbearably sad poem about a bitch whose puppies were thrown into a river to drown, which he knew in both Serbian and Russian. *Sobaka* – the Russian word for a dog – still sounds incredibly sad to me because of that poem. My mother's range was extensive, but she was fonder of reciting prose, and particularly the final lines of *Père Goriot* by Balzac, where an elderly man – whose two daughters had married into the aristocracy and abandoned him – is buried at the expense of a poor student. After a while, we were all able to reel off the inscription on old Goriot's gravestone without prompting. I am not sure if my mother's fondness for that particular scene came from an unconscious desire to see her daughters marry aristocrats and abandon her, or from her regret that she had left her own parental home in eastern Serbia to marry my father, or – and this was most likely – from her pure love of pathos. Mother was the only person I knew who actually *listened* to the words of pop songs on the radio and cried: particularly when the songs were about leaving home, lost loves, nostalgia and regrets in general. This used to annoy my father, a rational soul, no end. At times, we had a moratorium on music with words in our house, until I found my mother crying to the sounds of Saint-Saëns's *Swan*. Then we realized it was pointless and let her be.

My Montenegrin grandmother used to recite one or two classics of children's poetry and a vast selection of epic ballads, with a strong preference for blood and gore in both. Beheadings, impalings, the pulling out of hearts and livers: that was the substance of Granny's poetry. I still remember a Turkish hero, Musa, slain by the Christian Prince Marko, who was so brave it turned out he had two hearts and a double ribcage. Granny's other favourite was poetry about women's suffering, but she was no suffragette. In one verse, a mother of a small baby is immured in the foundations of a fortress, her breasts still heavy with milk, which ran like white tears from the stone. In another, an elderly mother nurses the hand of her youngest son, dropped from the sky by a raven flying from a distant battlefield. My favourite Granny poem was the one about a woman who was wrongly accused of being unfaithful. To punish her, her husband ties her to the tails of four horses and dismembers her. When he realizes that she was innocent, he repents and builds a monastery at each of the places where a part of her body first fell. The couple are reunited in heaven; a Montenegrin take on Lady Chatterley, I guess.

—

In the four years between my move to London and her death, Granny wrote to me only once. It was a short letter, pencilled in a deliberate hand clearly unused to writing. She reminded me to visit my parents regularly and urged me to behave in a way which would not dishonour my lineage: no laughing in public places, no loud conversation, modesty in dress and in everything else. Granny wrote as though she was worried that, away from my father and my tribe, I might be in danger of succumbing to some ungodly excess. In her world, Montenegrins who lived apart from their tribes were notoriously prone to prodigal or licentious behaviour. Her prompting came not because she lacked confidence in me, but because she clearly believed that this was what a letter from a grandmother to her granddaughter should be like. It wasn't the place for frivolities of any kind. Although written in continuous lines, her letter was – from the first word to the last – a string of rhythmic pentameters, the verse of Serbian epic poetry.

———

Much later, I realized that poetry writing had, in fact, something in common with lactation. Prompted by some mental/hormonal/ godly arrangement, the poetry comes as if from nowhere and, if not written down, engorges a swollen chest to the point of unbearable pain. Eventually, the urgency begins to ease and the writing takes place just intermittently. It is at this point only that it can be abandoned. Then it dries up completely. The organs which create verse – the heart, the brain, the fingers, the stomach – retain a memory of how it was once done, but are no longer able to produce poetry. In fact, like lactation, poetry is something that my adopted culture – let's call it British – is not entirely sure about. While poetry writing is nothing to be ashamed of, it's certainly better done in the privacy of one's own home.

Au contraire, the Yugoslavia of my adolescence was still stuck in that nineteenth-century frame of mind from which emerged Byron, Shelley and Tennyson, the bards, the lechers and the poets laureate, great men to be adored and admired, rather than shy nursing mothers. In terms of poetic role models, I was slightly better off than a British child of my age would have been. There were poets everywhere and they were celebrated. Communists wrote poetry, and so did workers and peasants, and it was par for the course as far as members of the honest intelligentsia were concerned. Many of our greatest national figures were poets. They were commemorated in macho monuments, wielding swords and sitting on horses, streets were named after them: what's there to be shy about?

The Yugoslav poets of that era could be divided into two broad groups: the state-sponsored bunch and the outcasts. The first lot wore suits (and, if male, ties) and held responsible jobs in the media, publishing and arts administration. Their books tended to appear with 'big' publishers in leather- and cloth-bound volumes with gold-embossed lettering, and got adulatory reviews. The outcasts wore rarely washed bohemian clothes, had badly cut hair and were frequently in dire need of a good dentist. They tended to read more broadly and had the obvious advantage of no nine-to-five (or, as it was locally, seven-to-three) jobs to insert a modicum of discipline into their days. They were published by small presses, if at all, in slim volumes of thirty to forty poems at most. These volumes were frequently illustrated

by the author (naturally, the suits had no time for such frivolities). They were hardly ever reviewed. In fact, a review was
generally a bad thing, a sign that someone was out to get you,
normally under the orders of a hostile suit somewhere higher
up. These reviews themselves required a finely honed set of
interpreting skills if one was to divine whether the author was
on the way to jail or not. Some of the outcast bohemians had
excellent connections among Belgrade's pickpockets from
shared stints in local prisons. If you had a drink with a boho in
a local pub you never knew who was going to come up to
say hello.

There was some element of crossover between the two groups
– a member of the boho tribe would temporarily sober up and
get a haircut and a good job with a publisher for a few months or
years. Given abundant state subsidy, these jobs required no
financial *savoir-faire*, and the absence of managerial qualities
was not a problem. The nicely heated new offices would
normally become a kind of drop-in centre for a particular
coterie of bohos, whose books were suddenly all over the
publishing lists for the coming year, and the whisky purchased
for the meetings with sales-rep teams was drunk in no time.
Things never lasted, however, for any boho worth his salt would
usually make a boo-boo of a political kind, normally by

publishing a book of verse which could be interpreted *differently*. This resulted in the pulping of volumes and so-called 'informative' conversations with poetry-loving cops down at the central police station.

The suits also occasionally missed a trick, which was all too easy to do, particularly with allegorical poetry, and would join the bohos for a few months or years in driverless wilderness. You could always tell a former suit in a group of bohos: their skin was too healthy, they got drunk too easily and they had regular, stable families consisting of one wife and one or two children. Even if quite a few bohos depended financially on wives with full-time employment, their marriages were usually shorter than one-book publishing deals. Both groups were equally lecherous and both groups were largely male. The suits were more used to getting women on a silver plate and the bohos to singing for their supper, but there was no difference in their basic assumption that writing poetry required more sex and seduction than tram driving.

Although there were very few women poets in those days, there was no shortage of female verse groupies who didn't write poetry themselves. They tended to come from the ranks of the literary proletariat: they were librarians, proofreaders, literature students and suchlike, temporarily bent on becoming famous as muses. Women poets as such were not unknown and, indeed, I can confirm that they were encouraged; but the overall atmosphere, not unlike a boozy men's club, was not too favourable for a writing female.

Those women who gained recognition through loss-leading literary magazines tended themselves to divide into bohos and suits, but the number of the latter was so tiny as to be practically non-existent. Most women poets kept ordinary day jobs, and had to wrestle with the sexual advances of men poets until such time as they were ready to become sexless mother figures revered as national monuments. In order to keep their jobs, even if of a bohemian persuasion, they allowed themselves only minor signs of eccentricity (a tilted hat, a floor-skimming skirt, a chain-smoking habit), and – unlike their male colleagues – never waited for decay to develop to the point where they had to have their front teeth extracted.

All in all, I was too fond of creature comforts (good-looking, tall and well-dressed young men included) ever seriously to consider a poetic career. However, I was not to know that when the verse started pouring out. The schools I attended needed and encouraged young poets – for inclusion in school magazines and yearbooks, participation in school poetry festivals, and all manner of other festive events. There were too many birthdays of famous people, anniversaries of battles and revolutions, name-days and openings of institutions. All needed a celebratory line or two, preferably in rhyme.

One of the nicest things about being a poet in socialist Yugoslavia was the idea that poetry mattered. State subsidy enabled poetry magazines to flourish and each two-horse town had a poetry festival all of its own. You could take part in those without having to pay five pounds for the first submission and two-fifty for each subsequent one, as you do in Britain, and I frequently did. By the time I was twenty-three, I had built a reputation as a moderately known poet, with a string of publications, one or two poetry prizes and regular high-profile readings on television poetry programmes. (I am not sure if even BBC4 would dare to schedule these in Britain.) I also developed admirable skills for rejecting excited poetic suitors with stories of boyfriends of long standing, although in a short while I began to feel distinctly bored after any stretch of time in the more mundane world of civvy street, where men generally tried to control their passions. I was aiming to publish a collection of my poems, which was more difficult, but not entirely beyond reach. Thank God I never succeeded in that particular effort.

The young poet

There was an annual competition for the publication of a first book by a young poet which normally attracted quite a lot of media attention. It had to, for journalists were under orders to cultivate young poets at the juncture where they could still be encouraged to turn into fully blown suits. My manuscript was short-listed and then rejected and I went to see the poetry editor, whose sad duty it was to have to explain rejection to all of us near-misses without discouraging us en masse. The poetry editor himself was a well-known provincial, neo-surrealist poet, and the main organizer of a number of quite outrageous 'happenings' around town, with a ridiculous name (as though his parents sensed the neo-surrealist angle even at birth). 'It's a fine collection, Vesna, mature well beyond your young years,' he said, welcoming me into a tiny, smoke-filled office on the first floor of an apartment block in a side street just off the main drag.

My poetry could hardly have failed to register as 'mature well beyond my young years' when it was full to bursting with the most recherché inter-textual allusions while at the same time brimming with references to the wilder kind of carnal experience, which was, I hardly need to say, derived largely from book reading (that early encounter with DHL had to leave an imprint somewhere, I guess). 'Fine collection, indeed, but lacking any sense of irony. You take yourself too seriously, my dear,' he continued, hitting the nail on the head. (All my poetic idols, from Alfred, Lord Tennyson, to Milan Rakic, took themselves very seriously indeed: grand, erudite and full of self-love was what I aimed to be.) 'How about a drink now, my dear child?' the editor punch-lined. I had to meet my 'boyfriend' immediately.

———

The themes of my poetry could be broadly divided into two subcategories: one, melancholy, self-indulgent love poetry; the other, Brechtian, rebellious, satirical and political. (The latter was likely to get me into trouble eventually, if I didn't watch it.) My earliest successful poems – successful in the sense of getting into print – were social-observational. However, I continued to write love poetry even when I was most certainly not in love with anyone. One of the earliest poems, entitled 'I Cried Like a Red Poppy in a Field of Wheat' and written when I was barely six, reveals all the characteristics of the genre which I was to polish and perfect through many years of wrestling with my melancholy, self-indulgent teenage muse.

I was particularly fond of penning what I now call a Penelope poem. In it, the female poetic subject is longing for an absent male, who is – normally because of some *force majeure* – obliged to go on travelling for years, leaving the said (sad) subject condemned to waiting, which she does, doggedly and faithfully, knitting, weaving, picking flowers, whatever. While the male subject is most often a known lover, he is sometimes as yet unmet (Penelope promises to recognize him when he finally decides to turn up). He is often just an ordinary male person with some special qualities, but he can equally have pseudo-religious powers: Jesus-like, omnipresent and all-knowing, and good beyond comprehension.

In many of these poems, the female who waits (the waitress) assumed a sexual authority, experience and world-weariness which the author arguably did not possess. Imagine sonnets written by Lady Caroline Lamb and you wouldn't be far off: while Byron is off in Missolonghi, what's the girl to do but write poetry? Throughout my late teens I used to show manuscripts to boyfriends, who tended to be unbothered by the fact that the poems were obviously not about them, and sometimes got rather too excited by the promise of adventure the verse contained.

By the time I hit my early twenties, I decided, in Marxist parlance, to wed theory and practice more closely, and began to affect the appearance of an incipient bohemian. I smoked filterless little cigarettes, allegedly favoured by Joseph Vissarionovich, which went very well with tiny glasses of grappa as strong as absinthe, a black duffel coat, a short crop (I was almost as breathless as Jean Seberg) and *an affaire du coeur* with Andrei, a white-haired literary scholar some thirty years older than me, who was not very interested in my poetry but immensely concerned to ensure that I didn't keep a diary.

He was so fond of lecturing that he couldn't really stop himself, and I loved that. Over the three years which followed, I learned more from him than from the entire university department at which I was studying. In the midst of it all, I suddenly stopped writing poetry, which pleased him no end, for, although he lived for the poetry of the past, he always seemed to find living poets slightly embarrassing, perhaps because he believed that the noblest emotions are the ones we repress. Soon afterwards I started two-timing him with a boy of my age and left, but continued to check out his books as they appeared, every year just before the book fair, hoping that one would be dedicated to me. The urge to be inspirational was, for a long while, much greater than the urge to be inspired, which is, perhaps, a woman thing. The strangest aspect of it all is that, in spite of spending literally hours and hours together, and most of them quite alone, we kissed only once. The man remains an enigma.

My greatest measurable achievement as a poet turned out to be taking part in the celebration of Comrade Tito's ninety-second birthday, or what would have been his ninety-second birthday had he not chosen to die just before his eighty-eighth. (During the lull before the storm of steel which shook my homeland in the nineties, 'official' Yugoslavia practised a strange form of necrophilia towards its erstwhile president for life.) In my household, the preparations had been debated for days. The discussion did not focus so much on the advisability of taking part, or the choice of poem – *that* would have been too rational; rather, we argued incessantly about what exactly I was going to wear. One had to think about the fact that the event was taking place before a live audience of 30,000 which gathered annually at a football stadium for the big day, people for whom I would represent no more than a distant blob of colour, and a further couple of million or so half-hearted TV viewers who were still watching the show out of a habit acquired in the long afternoon of Yugoslav socialism. For them, my poem would be – like the Archbishop of Canterbury's sermon at Lady Diana's wedding to Prince Charles – most probably a suitable window for a 'tea or pee' break. (No advertising was allowed to spoil the event.)

The exact outfit was the subject of heated arguments between myself, my mother, an assortment of relations and anyone else who cared to contribute. There was never a shortage of opinion, free of charge, in my neighbourhood. I was not really sure. One day I was certain it would be a pair of jeans with a white T-shirt and a pair of Converse All-Star trainers. (Blue or red *starke*, as they were called in Serbo-Croat, were the uniform footwear of my *lycée* clan.) My mother prepared to commit suicide. Next day I dreamed of a little black dress and Audrey Hepburn hair. Mother and the director of the show protested that black was highly inappropriate and suggested red. 'Your colour,' said my mother. '*Our* colour,' said the director. 'Peasant,' mumbled my sister. She used the feminine form of the noun. There was no doubt that she had me in mind. Only peasants wrote poetry anyway. (The word *peasant*, with its full power of character assassination, is not really translatable into English. It was neither here nor there as far as the real peasantry were concerned, but a poisoned dart if directed at a Belgrade student of letters.) Red, black or white, it made no difference. Writing poetry was not cool. Not unless sung, accompanied by no more than a single instrument, and even then only in alternative clubs with audiences in double digits. I couldn't count on my sibling's advice.

Finally, the die was cast. It was to be a labour of love – literally hours of painstaking embroidery – by Olga, a formidable raven-haired, blue-eyed Montenegrin, who was hoping to become my mother-in-law one day, but sadly never would. My *presque-belle-mère* smoked fragrant cigarettes and produced sweetmeats and cups of bitter coffee on little scalloped silver trays throughout the long sessions of fittings and gossip which preceded the big event. She was the kind of woman I might have loved to have been in a different life, in a different world. Feminine to the core yet iron-willed, she was the Montenegrin equivalent of a Southern belle or a Sicilian princess, with ivory-smooth skin, high cheekbones and smoky, deliberate speech. The clothes she dreamed up for me reflected the sensual grandeur of a life she wished for her children but which I, definitely, was never going to lead. It was a life marked by subtle scents, jewellery and expensive clothes never worn more than once.

Olga lived in a large apartment with sunny, wide balconies overlooking the Sava river, with her two children and husband, a director of a large agricultural consultancy, who spent much of his time in the Soviet Far East. The walls of the apartment were decorated with dozens of needlework reproductions of Old Masters and an assortment of Wiehler 'Gobelin tapestries' in ornate ormolu frames. Years ago, her children embellished many of the Wiehlers with stickers which she never bothered to remove. Anselm Feuerbach's *Iphigenia* gazed towards distant horizons dotted with low-flying US bomber planes, and a gargoyle stuck out a mischievous tongue from behind Empress Sissi of Austria, resplendent in her long buttermilk-coloured evening gown, a scene which uncannily evoked her end by the hand of an Italian assassin on the shores of Lake Geneva.

Olga's ornate salon was, for days on end, the nerve centre of feverish planning for my big day. Every aspect of my appearance was discussed in detail and dozens of possible outfits and hair-styles analysed and rejected. Finally, it was decided that I would walk on stage in a wine-coloured shirt of gossamer-thread chiffon, revealing a *charmeuse* camisole of the same colour. The skirt was made to measure from expensive woollen material purchased especially from a clothier on Via della Spiga in Milan by one of my aunts. The same aunt produced a pair of silk stockings and a pair of patent-leather shoes in a box lined with midnight-blue velvet. I felt like a porcelain doll dressed up by a gaggle of excited eight-year-old girls, showered with luxurious items they would never have dreamed of wearing themselves. Around my neck was a necklace of Ohrid pearls, from the deep lake of that name in Yugoslav Macedonia, worn back to front. Its ornate clasp was more suited to the occasion than the silver cross at the front, bearing the date of my grandparents' wedding and under it, in Cyrillic letters so tiny that they could only be read with a magnifying glass, 'Take me with you and we will run together', from the Song of Songs.

My Communist Party membership card

The stadium was full. Thousands of people filled the stands in an atmosphere which was in many ways the quintessence of the South Slav communist state. As it lay dying, the evening's event represented one of the final twitches. The audience consisted largely of young, jeans-and-T-shirt-clad people, looking in every respect like a large, good-natured football or rock-concert crowd, but with the volume turned right down. On the grass pitch, translucent green under dozens of powerful reflector lights, hundreds and hundreds of children, wearing colour-coordinated overalls and waving multicoloured ribbons, turned their heads towards me. An amazing, unreal silence fell on the crowd like a blanket.

I began to read my poem. My voice rose towards the indigo-coloured night sky beyond the reflector lights against the sound of a Schumann piano concerto. Only the voice was not mine. Or, rather, it was mine, but it wasn't live. I was simply opening my mouth, an expensive little goldfish dressed in raspberry, lip-synching to a tape which had been recorded in a studio deep in the bowels of Radio Belgrade a day or so earlier. No one was supposed to know that. I was too far away for anyone in the audience to notice, and the TV cameramen were told to go easy on close-ups. 'To prevent any accidents,' the event's director said. I took that to mean accidents involving such seismic degrees of stage fright as would make one unable to utter a word. Dead on arrival in front of the 30,000. Now I wonder if what he meant was something altogether more sinister, such as saying things that one was not meant to say, things which might lose him a job and me my future. Or not saying a thing.

My lip-synching did not even seem particularly strange in the context of the birthday party for a man who had already been dead for four years. For a while Yugoslavs continued to celebrate the day in the traditional manner, with torches lit from eternal flames relayed around the country by handsome athletes, young workers and bright students, in a well-rehearsed marathon which was the first item on the news bulletins throughout the spring. The longer it was since his demise, the more there was to celebrate. Like the widow of a murdered Sicilian Mafia don, the country clung to his memory in an incongruous mixture of mourning and *décolletage*, as if knowing that a collective nervous breakdown would follow once the ritual was no longer observed.

There was something fated, something unavoidable about me being Tito's posthumously chosen poet, even if I had never met him while he was alive. He and I had been narrowly missing each other since May 1969, when I was selected by my teachers, as a bright seven-year-old, to head a delegation of pioneers from my primary school in Dedinye on a trip to the White Palace.

Mine was a privileged school full of good-looking kids, in the right kind of neighbourhood, populated by army officers and party apparatchiks. It was a safe bet for this kind of event. Seeing us, Comrade Tito could not fail to observe the contentedness of Yugoslavia's youth. I was supposed to hand him a bunch of flowers and give a four-line speech (composed by me and carefully vetted God knows where). Three days before the event, while practising a particularly difficult manoeuvre on my rollerskates, I fell on a rough piece of concrete by the garages behind our block of flats and broke my arm. The headmistress promptly declared that a plaster cast was inappropriate for even a member, let alone the head, of the delegation. Somebody else was to read my speech. I was ordered to stay at home, bitterly disappointed.

———

Tito's main residence was on Uzhichka Street, a quiet road of neoclassical villas with carefully tended gardens, just down the road from the block of flats in which my father, recently employed by the Yugoslav National Army General Staff, was awarded the use of a one-bedroom apartment (pure luxury after our two-room bathroomless house: we were downwardly mobile for decades, but Dedinye marked the point when the tide might have begun to turn). With its wide pavements and hardly any traffic, Uzhichka Street was one of my favourite cycling and roller-skating grounds. Surly policemen would frequently ask me to get off my cycle and step to one side to watch a cavalcade of motorcycles and dark limousines turn through the heavy gates of Tito's villa, flanked by hand-picked guards officers in aquamarine coats and shiny black boots, bearing black guns in their white gloved hands. I often detected Tito's carefully coiffed and tinted reddish-brown head of hair behind the dark glass. Once or twice, he turned towards me and watched.

Later on, living in a different part of town and going to a different school, I'd often form part of the crowd bussed in to line the wide boulevards in order to greet him and his visiting dignitaries returning from the airport, all of us happy to be getting a day off school and armed with little paper flags (a Yugoslav tricolour with a red star and a different one, appropriate for the foreign guest and treasured by the school collector-nerds). We waved cheerfully for what was never more than a momentary glimpse after a couple of hours' wait at the kerbside. The flags were particularly plentiful when the visitors happened to be from one of the friendly non-aligned countries: Comrade Tito and Comrade Sukarno of Indonesia, Comrade Tito and Comrade Indira Gandhi of India, Comrade Tito and

Comrade Nasser of Egypt, Comrade Tito and Comrade Yasser Arafat of the Palestine Liberation Organization, etc. Our president's uniforms were shown to their best advantage against the colourful outfits of the Third World: the saris, the sarongs and the dashikis emphasized by contrast the details of the fine tailoring so beloved by the dandy of the socialist world. I can see him even now, smelling of cigars and eau-de-cologne and lording it like a male version of the British Queen at one of her Commonwealth jamborees. He was able to bring happiness unto the nations without her imperial burdens.

———

My poem was the fourth in the cycle of sonnets about Jesus (it was, as it turns out, one of the last five or six poems I was ever going to write), but Our Lord was not referred to by name anywhere. The melancholy miracle maker of my youthful verse, could, at a push, have been anyone. The organizers of the birthday do might have been aware of this in a much shrewder way than I would have given them credit for when I was originally approached to submit a selection of my poetry for consideration. The approach itself caused a lot of anguish. Was I going to do it and, more importantly, could I refuse? Why had I been selected? OK, I had a full set of teeth and a full head of hair, as well as a fine voice and broadcasting experience, all of which amounted to a thoroughly unusual combination in Yugoslav poetic circles. Nonetheless, mine was hardly a name of which anyone but the most avid reader of small magazines would have been aware. Let's face it, I was as close to being a poetic nonentity as a winner of a few poetry competitions could be.

It turned out that one of the event's directors was a fan. Having first met me at a provincial poetry competition when I was seventeen, he had taken a sporadic interest in my writing ever since, and kept a small selection of my poems in his office at the TV station where he worked (also bombed to smithereens, my manuscripts and all, by NATO in 1999). Politically, he was, I believe, a Titoist of the old guard, an old-fashioned communist idealist, and personally this side of nice – a rare trait in TV directors anywhere – that is, nice to me at least. He'd take me out for an occasional lunch or a walk by the Danube, and we'd have long conversations about poetry (he was a poet himself – an über-suit), life, death, men, women, the meaning of life, Herzegovina. To be of old Belgrade stock but also from Herzegovina was for me the winning combination – a bit like having a house in Mayfair and an old family castle in the wildest part of the Scottish Highlands – but that was perhaps only because I was of the same stock myself.

111

Although he lingered above it from time to time, he never crossed the line which I had, as he might well have suspected, drawn in the sand around me. I enjoyed his attentions and he enjoyed bestowing them on me, and was, to his eternal credit, wise enough to keep that enjoyment alive for a long while. If I were his wife (he had one), I would have been mildly annoyed, but not unduly worried. I was a good girl, I think. That is perhaps the main reason why I was chosen and that is perhaps why I had agreed to indulge him, even when every sinew in my body recoiled from Tito's funerary fête. That, and the insistence of my mother and assorted aunts, for whom the idea of reading a poem in front of a live audience of 30,000, and TV audiences in their millions, was not one that should be turned down lightly. The fact that my reading would be sandwiched between the appearances of two of the sexiest bands in Yugoslavia did not seem at all incongruous to me; it was, in fact, what my female friends envied the most. I shared a taxi home from the rehearsals with the legendary lead singer of White Button of Sarajevo, with the hips of Mick Jagger and the hairdo of Jimi Hendrix, on at least a couple of occasions, and discovered that he had a habit of kissing goodbye most sexily, although I am not entirely sure that he would have remembered me, even a month later. We were the most unlikely of fellow-travellers.

112

That the event was kitsch, a peculiarly Yugoslav kind of kitsch – combining punk, poetry and sport, like a toaster with an in-built barometer and alarm clock – was perfectly clear to me even then. A proper Eastern Bloc country would have had a poet of a much greater stature than me and a bunch of opera singers of world repute, rather than a literature student wedged between a Croatian version of the Sex Pistols in black leather and ageing Bosnian rockers. Down on the pitch, there was none of the muscle-and-tone blond coordination familiar from similar German events filmed by Leni Riefenstahl, only rows of kids who cheerfully moved about waving their brightly coloured ribbons, lucky to have been given a couple of weeks off school for rehearsals.

With the hindsight of twenty years, the whole event seems perhaps much more tightly controlled than it appeared to me then. My voice was not my own. There was no place for improv-isation, not an inch of space for manoeuvre. As I was sitting on the special guest platform, surveying the crowds after my historic non-reading and then enjoying a big congratulatory hug from Zagreb's handsome response to Sid Vicious (his leather jacket rubbing noisily against my chiffon blouse), a familiar face appeared just behind me.

'I just wanted to say hello,' whispered Zoran, a school friend whom I barely recognized. His long blond Jim Morrison locks were now trimmed into the shortest possible crop. 'Hey, Zocky, how's tricks? Who are you with?' I chirped, high on the taste of my newly acquired stardom. 'The police academy,' he answered. 'I am a student there now. We are all around you tonight.'

5

PETER THE GREAT, PETER THE FEARLESS AND OTHER ROMANCES

I am a reluctant accountant of the heart. I've loved some men and others have loved me; and then there was a handful of times when loving and loving back kept the see-saw in balance, my feet in the air and my eyes on the sky. No life's story now seems complete without ledgers of affection, yet they create hierarchies which betray and deceive. Time lengthens some horizons and foreshortens others. There are memories which haunt and memories which sleep like babies in little white coffins. With passing years, a single kiss can acquire more meaning than months of naked skin.

Andrei stood up from an armchair in his unlit, freezing room. French windows flooded with moonlight looked down on to a narrow, icy lane. The headlamps from passing cars pierced thick curtains of snow like searchlights. Pools of amber light lapped on the high ceiling for a few moments and withdrew. The entire building vibrated with stifled sounds of music. Across the road, the Belgrade Philharmonic Orchestra was rehearsing by candle-light. The city was frozen in the middle of a blackout, without electricity and heating. Trams and trolleybuses stood aban-doned in their tracks.

The Yeti woman walking through the snow drifts was me. I wore two vests, a checked flannel shirt, a heavy woollen jumper, two pairs of stockings, green moleskin dungarees and red snow boots, and – over all of that – a mink coat of syrup-coloured pelts, a birthday present from my parents, and a red fox-fur hat with earflaps drawn tightly under my chin. Around my shoulders, I wrapped my mother's silver stole. The dead head of an animal with ruby glass eyes hung on my chest, biting its own tail. It was eighteen below zero, but I was also playing the Arctic queen. Nothing and no one could make me unhappy in those days. I ran on my own power supply.

The doorbell did not work. I knocked while shaking the snow off my boots and my hat. I removed nothing when I stepped inside. My frozen breath hung in the air. A row of thin yellow candles threw flickering shadows on hundreds of book spines in glass cases. The room was full of ghosts. Andrei came towards me and I stretched my mittened hand out to greet him, but he took a further step which made the handshake impossible. His white hair glistened in semi-darkness. The temperature was so low that I could feel the icy crescent shapes of each of my twenty nails.

He took his glasses off and carefully put them down on his desk in a gesture which somehow managed to be dizzyingly intimate. I heard my heartbeat and the sound of gold wire coming to rest on the surface of wood. I kept my eyes open when he closed his and lowered his head towards me. Our kiss lasted barely ten seconds: this was the first time I really touched Andrei, even though we had spent hours poised over books in this very room. 'Your lips taste of snow,' he said, still using the formal *you*.

Andrei's jacket smelled of mothballs, and his fine, smooth, old-man's skin of baby soap and talcum powder. This was not an erotic kiss. It was not the beginning of anything. He took a step back and picked his glasses up. I was determined to pretend that nothing unusual had happened. I sat down in my chair, in which, over the three years which preceded this evening, I had learned everything that I will ever know about reading books; reading was – it turns out – my most enduring passion. In the whole of Belgrade, in the whole of the Balkans perhaps, there was no better interpreter of books than this small bespectacled man; and in the rest of the world it seemed to me that no more than a handful were his equals.

When I became a teacher of literature, I sometimes took his books out of the university library in Bloomsbury, where they languished, uncherished and unborrowed, in their modest Serbian covers. It was a mystery that the library had them at all. As I prepared my lectures, I remembered Andrei's voice. He'd bend over a book and, jabbing a word with his finger, exclaim: 'Here, Vesna, here is what we were looking for.' I knew that he was attracted to me and I also sensed that our reading sessions gave him a thrill of self-denial. What I was not ready to admit, not even to myself, was that I enjoyed playing with him in the safety of his self-control. I'd lean too far forward or hold his gaze a second too long, fine-tuning my skills of seduction, as cruel and as ignorant of hurt as a young animal can be. Reading with Andrei was always both dangerous and thrilling, like holding a key to the fairy-tale chamber which might unleash the hurricane. Kissing him felt safe and a bit sad, but it was a taste I had to learn about too. The virtuous make the poorest of readers.

I had crossed the dark city to get to his study and would have to cross it again to return home. The journey was my parting gift. We both knew that I was never going to visit him again. Not because of that kiss: it was one of the gentlest I have ever received. I was the upstart demigod in a Greek story, standing in the door frame with the fire I had stolen. In my dreams, I had tried being both Andrei's wife and his lover, and neither seemed possible at all, but as his student, God, yes, as his student, I was beyond compare.

I've always had a certain chameleon quality, which came from never really knowing who I was. If I fell in love, I'd tackle the man as a study project and begin emulating everything he did. I'd catch up with his favourite films and favourite books – however stupid – and start watching, and indeed sometimes even playing, his favourite sports. I'd adopt his taste in music and food, his way of dressing and his accent. I can still remember the look of horror on my parents' face one summer, when – because of a blond air-traffic controller from Dubrovnik – I suddenly began to elongate my vowels in the way they do on the Adriatic coast. For a long while, it seemed that only by becoming someone else could I truly be myself. Wise men found this unnerving, simpler ones admired our uncanny similarities.

Until I started growing that wild piece of flesh in my breast – my *tumourchich* – I was always happy to turn into a lizard or a leaf, as the situation required. Then, at forty-one, and perhaps for the first time in my life, I suddenly felt too tired for such games. I no longer really cared whether anybody liked me or not. Then I discovered I was no longer able to change colour at all. I stretched my white body on my big green leaf, a bald, wounded caterpillar. I was free.

———

In the early eighties, Petar was one of the top students of economics at Belgrade University and a prominent member of the Socialist Youth League. He was two years older than me, thin and tall, with curly black hair and a melancholy, narrow face which could have been painted by El Greco. There was an intensity about him which was difficult to pin down. I called him Pierre, after Pierre Bezukhov in Tolstoy's *War and Peace*, which means – very approximately – Peter the Earless. This name suited him very well. Bezukhov was a loser, and I sensed the same instinct for losing a game in Petar, even though, superficially, one might have said just the opposite. He was a political star in the making and I was a flighty kid, dreaming of literary fame. Underneath, however, he was as vulnerable as a reed and I had a steel armature.

I first met Petar at a local poetry competition. I remember being struck, as if by a flash of recognition, by a long, clever face in the audience. I've only ever felt that sort of thing – hinges closing, a complicated piece of jigsaw falling into its proper place – two or three times in my forty-odd years, and each time it happened, I was sure I was never going to feel anything like it again. We took the tram back into town. Halfway down the Boulevard of the Revolution, the longest street in Belgrade, Petar put his hand on my shoulder. It was as simple as that.

He called me Françoise, which was only in part meant to reflect my incorrigible pomposity. I took myself very seriously indeed. In fact, the name was much more the product of circumstance. Most of our evenings began at the gate of my French school on top of Prince Milosh Street, from where we walked slowly downhill towards the ugly spaghetti junction which separated central Belgrade from its southern suburbs.

Speaking French for a couple of hours, in a converted bourgeois apartment in a mansion block overlooking one of Belgrade's busiest intersections, always made me unaccountably happy. My chameleon nature simply shone when it came to

121

learning foreign languages, which I seemed to master without effort, as if by osmosis. Before I was twenty-five, I had studied Latin, Greek, Old Church Slavonic, English, French, Russian, Bulgarian, Italian and Japanese, with varying degrees of determination and success, but I loved speaking French more than any other language. After each class, I practically glided down the grand marble staircase to meet 'Pierre'. The only foreign language he spoke was Russian. This fitted the roles I saw us in – the princess and the commissar – very well indeed.

Belgrade University, 1930s

My French teachers, Madame Mimitza and Madame Foni – the former blonde and almost Scandinavian in appearance, the latter Athenian by birth, with glossy dark hair and black-rimmed glasses – both seemed fantastically, unattainably French to me. In fact, they were more French than most French women ever manage to be. It takes a certain *je ne sais quoi* which only elegant women in the East seem to possess to attain that kind of Frenchness, like the teaspoonful of sugar which makes savoury foods taste more of themselves.

At one stage in my teens, I made conscious efforts to be more ladylike myself. I cut my hair in a straight bob and wore twin-sets, tartan skirts and little ballet pumps in a way which pleased my mother immensely. Then I began seeing the captain of my school basketball team and went back into jeans and trainers. The captain was six foot six. I can still remember burying my nose into the middle of a big fleecy number on his team shirt smelling deliciously of sweat when we embraced after his sporting triumphs. One December evening, while I was suffering from a very bad episode of pneumonia, he came to visit me at my bedside with a fragrant little posy of dwarf violets in his enormous hands, and enquired whether I was planning to be back on my feet in time for the New Year. When I told him that such a speedy recovery seemed highly unlikely, he suggested that it might be better if we parted at that point. He wanted a girlfriend for New Year's Eve and, as I was obviously not cooperating, there was just enough time to find a new one. I was so feverish I couldn't even summon the strength to get up and kick him out of the house. One learns a lot about fair play by dating sportsmen.

I went back to French bobs and twinsets and gave up my own, admittedly not at all promising, career in high-school basketball. In the best traditions of socialist education, my school encouraged sporting prowess as much as any scientific or artistic skills. Even at the university, one couldn't sign up for exams without proof of participation at the weekly skating or swimming sessions and the annual two-kilometre race at the hippodrome. I chose shooting practice, which was more useful than skating and lacked the painful associations of basketball. By the time I met Petar, I was quite a markswoman.

My French school was, in many ways, one of the most selective institutions in socialist Belgrade. Parents were interviewed and vetted as thoroughly as prospective students. To get me and my sister a place, my father expended his entire reservoir of charm upon Madame Dora, who was in charge of admissions. He knew that his work for the army might be a drawback (it was that kind of institution), but his handsome manner won the day.

The school's recitals were legendary and quite a few of our classes were devoted to rehearsals and preparation. One year, I polished the lines from Aragon's *La Rose et le Réséda* until each elision and each emphasis fell in its proper place, and Madame Mimitza told me that I sounded 'almost French', the greatest compliment of all. The French ambassador and the cultural attaché always sat in the first row with representatives of the old, French-educated Belgrade elite. Even the French President, Giscard d'Estaing, turned up with his wife at one of our performances. Each vase in the school was full of gardenias and there were trays of pastel-coloured almond mignons on every side table. The grand piano was tuned and polished for the occasion. Overexcited boys and girls in starched white collars and patent-leather shoes responded to the President's questions in deliberate, careful French. Madame Mimitza and Madame Foni hovered behind smiling anxiously.

After my first stay in Paris, paid for by the French Ministry of Culture as an award for an essay in French entitled, appropriately, 'Why I love France', I affected a Parisian accent and said things like *shai pas* instead of *je ne sais pas*, as though I was brought up in an apartment on Ile de la Cité and had not just spent three weeks in a hostel opposite Père Lachaise cemetery. How I loved France! There was never any aplomb in my boring English school, where my Anglophobe but practically minded parents sent me twice a week from the age of seven to the age of eighteen. We were confined to dire pieces about Stratford-upon-Avon and Stonehenge and the same old excerpts from Dickens again and again. The teachers did not seem to care that most of the students were interested only in things American and were adopting the most implausible American accents, picked up in local cinemas. How come I ended up on this island, speaking English all the time?

Quite what Petar, a socialist and a true egalitarian, saw in my breathless, Francophone snobbery is anyone's guess. The two of us walked, argued about politics and occasionally stopped to exchange passionate kisses. You hardly ever see people kissing like that on the streets of London, but in southern Europe, where young people continue to live with their parents throughout the years of yearning, it is a common sight. The thick, dark crowns of lime trees which lined Prince Milosh Street were full of sparrows chirping dementedly, and the wind-screens of cars parked underneath were dotted with guano, like oversized snowflakes. In late spring and early summer, the smell of exhaust fumes from battered buses mixed with the sickly fragrance of lime blossom. The street was a canyon, its walls made up of large, ugly edifices: embassy buildings, ministries and government headquarters. It was about as intimate as walking down Whitehall in London or Pennsylvania Avenue in Washington. Numerous little guards huts, no bigger than telephone boxes, lined the pavements. In some of these, policemen in tight blue uniforms sat listening to their radios or eating hotdogs. In others, young soldiers in heavy grey overcoats stood forlornly with guns on their shoulders.

Embassies of the more or less friendly socialist countries had large panels with photographs showing off economic and cultural achievements. Everyone on those panels seemed blissfully happy, but the cumulative effect was always depressing. Western embassies tended to have a folded flag in the lobby, like a forgotten beach parasol, and a large photo of their president. If the country in question was a monarchy, the display seemed more familiar: a painting of a glum middle-aged woman with a tiara, very much like Comrade Jovanka, or a finely manicured chap in an elaborate uniform, like our own Comrade Tito. Ideological differences notwithstanding, these were fellow Ruritanians.

On one of our walks, I entertained Petar with a theory, tailored entirely to suit my Francophilia, that 'nice' countries had red, white and blue flags, while 'nasty' ones always included yellow. This theory reflected my political maturity. I was one of those people who always read the newspapers from the back, stopping two-thirds of the way through, just after the book pages. I made a conscious effort to know as little about politics as possible.

Petar was the exact opposite. He didn't just read the newspapers, he *read* them. He knew what each minute shift in government signified, and why – in a well-rehearsed speech – Comrade So-and-So described someone as a demagogue, a technocrat or an opportunist. He knew why pauses for applause were scheduled after particular rhetorical flourishes in the speech but not after others. In those days, the most inconspicuous turns of phrase hid major power struggles. 'There are doubters in our society,' someone would announce grandly, and suddenly – as if on cue – doubters would be rooted out, fired from their jobs or sent to prison, as appropriate to the magnitude of the doubt they harboured.

Petar was also one of the first people I knew to mutter darkly about unseen powers which were working to break Yugoslavia apart. He seemed very fond of Yugoslavia. I liked the place too – it was my country, after all – but cared much less about whether its constituent parts remained together or not, so long as Belgrade went on more or less as usual. At that stage, I still believed that given the freedom to vote most Yugoslavs would vote Green and focus on cutting petrol emissions. I could not have imagined that, soon after I left the country, it would be in the hands of people like Slobodan Milosevic or Franjo Tudjman. I was barely aware that such men existed. I didn't think that anyone could be so foolish as practically to ask to be bombed by the West. Nor did I assume that the Western armies would oblige. I'd underestimated the whole lot of them.

Given that members of my wider family – to count just the non-combatants – had been murdered by soldiers belonging to at least five different nationalities in the past hundred years or so, my optimism was astonishingly naive. I never paused to worry about my relations in Sarajevo, for example. What could happen to my uncle Mladen and his Croatian wife, or my cousin Danny and his Muslim wife? My plans for the future somehow always allowed for winters on the snow slopes around the Bosnian capital, followed by baked apples with walnuts and sour cherries in 'Egypt', the best patisserie in town.

It was in 'Egypt' that one of my cousins once exclaimed, laughing, 'I have a fine lot of Belgrade girls here, mash'Allah.' His moustache tipped with icing sugar spread across his face, revealing a row of shiny white teeth. 'And how much do you ask for those two sweet apples? I'll take them to Istanbul, so help me God,' retorted another beaming, moustachioed man. We tugged our cousin's sleeve in panic, worrying that he might really sell us. I now wonder whether we sold him in the end.

———

One evening, Petar and I stopped in front of Belgrade's River Navy headquarters at the bottom of Prince Milosh Street. We kissed until every one of the buses home went by. 'We can't go on like this, Petar,' I said, my voice breaking down after only seven words, although I had practised the speech all day. 'I am leaving you.' I opened my satchel full of French textbooks and, by way of explanation, produced a letter, or rather a collection of moderately censored extracts copied from my diary. I had suspected all along that I wouldn't have the nerve for an exegesis of what exactly had led me to this fork in the road, yet I felt I owed it to Petar.

He stood and read my document for the best part of ten minutes, giving very little away, then hugged me wordlessly – in what already felt like a different kind of embrace – and I caught my bus home. It then took me nearly a year before I stopped wanting to dial his number and to take every one of those 2,000-odd words back.

———

I recalled this particular evening as I watched the buildings between which Petar and I had stood burn on *Channel Four News* in 1999. They were hit by precision bombs, together with almost all of the government headquarters but none of the many embassies on the street, in what seemed like the military equivalent of dentistry. My friend Ana, whose house stood just up the road from the Foreign Ministry, rang me in London the following morning – as I was leaving for a day of research at the British Library – to say that she had been woken up by rays of sunshine playing on her face. She was just thinking that she had left the blinds up when she realized that overnight a crack wide enough to let the light through had opened up in one of the walls.

The bombing had apparently sent her whole neighbourhood on the move downhill, towards the river. 'You must write to every British newspaper about this,' Ana said, displaying an astonishing lack of understanding about the way *real* democracy works. Fissures of this kind only ever feature on local news. Given that her building insurance excluded acts of war, that the bank which had underwritten it was bankrupt anyway and that her salary at Belgrade University amounted to just under thirty pounds a month, paid in two instalments – well, one could understand the state of mind she was in.

Ana's call had interrupted a chain of reminiscences brought about by aerial destruction, a very Balkan *à la recherche*. The girl who abandoned Petar might or might not have been me. Like a premeditated murder, it was an act both planned and sudden. Until it happened, I never thought I'd be able to go through with it. This is not to say that I have ever, for a moment, regretted my departure; just that I have, in the intervening years, lost touch with that girl who could – like NATO – destroy and create on a large scale while following an instinct no stronger than a distant whistle. I now wanted to know her again.

———

Petar and I were from different backgrounds. I never met either of his parents. In Petar's world, being introduced to your boyfriend's parents signified a stage in a relationship which we did not quite reach, the point of no return. He met both of mine. In my circles, meeting someone's parents was of relatively little consequence (even if they were inclined to weigh the pros and cons of even the most unlikely spousal 'candidate'). Mother and Father simply happened to be *en route* to the record collection or the kitchen. Mother, in particular, always made sure that she was *en route*. If all else failed, she'd turn up, without knocking, just inside my room door, with a silver tray. She usually couldn't knock because of her burden of homemade biscuits and heavy Bohemian glasses filled with Coca-Cola.

Mother taught us early on that the simpler the offering the more ornate the presentation needed to be. Hence crystal for Coke, a drink she despised, whereas caviar was best eaten off the back of your own hand. Not that any of my boyfriends were ever offered caviar, on or off the hand. Our occasional supply of Caspian Beluga, which often came in tins bearing the stamp of the Romanian diplomatic stores, was set aside for New Year's Eve, halfway through our Christmas fast (Orthodox Christmas being on 7 January). Since we were allowed no meat or dairy food, we relied on caviar and champagne – even if only Russkoe Shampanskoe – and this seemed the best way of fasting that anyone has ever come up with. My sister and I were permitted small glasses of sweet champagne as far back as I can remember. She got drunk on a thimbleful of Russkoe Shampanskoe when she was six, and sang her way into the New Year.

———

Petar's father was a cabinet-maker whose trade was killed off by the fashion for furniture from Slovenia, which first began to grip middle-class Yugoslav households in the late sixties. Most of the well-to-do families up and down the country owned one of about four different designs: Louis Quinze (at its most surreal when applied to wall-to-wall chipboard wardrobes known locally as *regali*), Bauhaus, rustic and 'contemporary'. The furniture was normally bought with extremely low-interest loans. Yugoslav yuppies were flush with money from the funds with which the West supported Comrade Tito in his hairdressing follies, to the annoyance of the entire Eastern Bloc. His crown was growing redder by the day.

One tended to feel instantly at home in a flat one had never visited before. Give or take a painting or an upright piano in the corner, everyone's dwelling was more or less the same. The marketing campaigns of the Slovene furniture industry, with happy couples opening the doors of richly carved bureaux to reveal brand-new colour television sets, also Slovene, and toasting each other with a glass of Slovene Riesling, left old-style cabinet-makers like Petar's father with few commissions. Slovenia was our California, the land we all wanted to live in, and the Slovenes lived on that dream.

Our own family furniture was a socialist take on Louis Quinze, my mother's choice. I've also seen it on TV in the study of the head of the Serbian Academy of Sciences and Arts, and, a decade later, in the living room of an alleged war criminal which was being ransacked by the UN police in what seemed like a futile attempt to find someone hiding under a small commode. The head of the academy had a large library; the war criminal's wife must have had a taste for crochet, for there were antimacassars everywhere, but the rooms were otherwise more or less identical to ours. I felt that, through furniture, I had a special path to understanding the world I came from. Whereas in the West the inexhaustible variety of interior design often manages to obscure surprising degrees of conformity, the enforced conformity of the society I grew up in concealed a bunch of eccentrics and sometimes downright madness. While the wives were crocheting, madmen were busily planning Armageddon.

———

Petar's mother was a Serb from Croatia, some years older than his father, a Croat concentration camp survivor, and a housewife. This last, a very rare thing, provoked in me a mixture of jealousy and pity. Socialist children tended to prefer parentless homes which were unsupervised until late in the afternoon, but envied the freshly prepared lunches and other comforts a *mother at home* implied. To my generation of kids, raised by women bus drivers and nuclear physicists, a *mother at home* tended to signify either extreme privilege or dire poverty.

In most respects, what someone might see as the class differences between Petar and me mattered little in our classless society; I was hardly the Duchess of Devonshire myself. Even money – or the absence of it – did not seem to matter very much. You didn't study comparative literature in the hope of making your first million before you were thirty. We barely needed any money at all.

We loved to sit in workmen's *kafane*, smoky boozers in which a drink cost only a few pence and no one we knew ever turned up. These places were staffed by surly waitresses in peep-toe canvas boots, *borosane*, designed to prevent varicose veins and quite possibly the ugliest footwear on earth. They were mandatory for workers in state-owned shops and hostelries. One of the waitresses would eventually come up to us, clutching an enormous leather wallet and dodging hands, stretched out from surrounding tables, which were bent on pinching her bottom. She'd say something along the lines of 'What's for you two lovebirds?' in a voice coarse from cigarette smoke. While the state worried about varicose veins, these women were inhaling the equivalent of three packets of cigarettes a day.

Petar and I were usually in the middle of a conversation about world politics. I said I had no interest in politics but I loved arguing with him and would often adopt a position which I thought might infuriate him, siding with some crazed bunch of nationalists in Spain or Sri Lanka who had just blown a few people up, simply in order to get him going. Arguing with Petar in the middle of a smoky *kafana* always managed to seem incredibly glamorous to me. He always gave each argument his best shot and would never give up until I conceded the point. Between the two of us, it was always 1917 all over again, the early snows of November danced in the air and Russia was ready to pull out of the war: the end of the world as I knew it. Except that I was about to escape to Paris and Petar was to ride the bullet train until the ice-pick got him. That's how it seemed anyway.

I'd light a Herzegovina, my favourite brand of cigarettes, and order a shot of *loza*, the fiery Montenegrin brandy made from vine leaves, and a glass of water: the kind of order which was practically a must for a self-respecting poet. During this particular phase I'd rather be seen dead than smoking Western cigarettes and drinking Western alcohol, with perhaps the sole exception of Gauloises, which – while undoubtedly Western – somehow seemed to have an Eastern heart. It wasn't that I was anti-Western, quite the opposite, but that, by the early eighties, the comrades had become so fond of whisky and American tobacco that self-respecting literature students like myself had no other option but to support the domestic product.

Sinking in my chair, I'd flick the ash with a devil-may-care attitude which belied the fact that, at that stage, I didn't dare light a cigarette within a two-mile radius of my home. (The concealment of my smoking kit in the lining of my duffel coat and furious mint-sucking on the bus home were part and parcel of going out.) I loved the Serbian folk music which often played on decrepit radios in Belgrade's *kafane*. The songs were about life, love and death, and could only have been written by people whose life experience was brutal and likely to be short. I rarely listened to that kind of music at home. It simply did not sound the same in Slovene Louis Quinze surroundings.

———

Not so long ago, I discovered that this kind of music, when played very loudly on my Walkman, eased the nausea which I felt when the long cannula went into my veins to deliver the three-weekly dose of chemotherapy. My stomach heaved while Epirubicin, the drug known as the Red Devil, coursed through my body, hopefully doing away with my cancer, but also with my fertility and my hair. Even as I write this – many weeks after this particular phase of treatment – my insides move towards my throat and saliva floods my mouth at the memory. It made sense that the Red Devil should come to the rescue of the Red Princess, and that the price he demanded should be high. Serbian singers cursed their mothers from my earphones: 'O Mother, O my cursed Mama, why did you give birth to me, when I have no luck at all?' Their wailing protected me from fellow patients around me, some hairless, some with blue ice-caps on their heads, some quietly sick, some crying, some eager to exchange cancer notes. We were all called brave, but we had no other choice. In the midst of all the suffering I was witnessing and feeling, I felt strangely elated by the songs which suddenly seemed to stand for the best of the world I came from. I too had given birth and was ready to be cursed in my own turn. There was nothing to be scared of any more.

It took me a long while to accept that I left Petar because I was jealous. There was never any sign that he was seeing someone else, but I am not given to that kind of jealousy anyway. I am a continental European, after all, not like your average product of the Anglo-Puritan stock, always either on the wagon or off, either in AA or in *delirium tremens*. I tend not to worry too much about rivals, so long as I can be convinced that I am the centre of the universe. The key here is in the word 'convinced', rather than objective reality, towards which I've always maintained a Baudrillard-like sense of scepticism. I gradually began to feel more and more bothered by the fact that I seemed to be only the centre of a minor galaxy of Petar's. There were other, inhabited galaxies around: his studies, his political activism and other, smaller things. I began to collect grievances like stamps. Soon nothing seemed right any more. I was preparing for take-off.

I suspect that Petar would not see our history quite in these terms. Eventually we became friends. One summer, we toured the monasteries of Kosovo with Simon, by then my English husband. In hot, crowded buses, trundling on dusty roads through yellowing crabgrass, Petar and I spoke English, a language he had picked up in the changing tides but in which he was not at all comfortable. We often preferred not being identified as Serbs. To be a Serb in the south was not dangerous – not yet at that stage – but it was increasingly unpleasant. The few Albanians we spoke to were thirsty for their own state. They maintained a fiery conviction in the justice of their cause. In the tragic story of Yugoslav dissolution, theirs was the most difficult chapter. They were wretchedly poor and did not even pretend loyalty to the South Slav state. Why should they have?

In the monasteries we visited, the tall figures of saints on frescoes had their eyes scratched out. The whiteness of their stares disconcerted me and I felt that they too were somehow unable to see past their own pain. We crossed into Macedonia, and with that crossing came a much greater sense of ease. We swam off rotting shallow boats in intense heat which hung like a curtain over the blue waters of Lake Ohrid. The mossy heights of Prokletije, the Accursed Mountains, threw dark shadows over the water from the southern, Albanian shore. Border patrol boats hovered in the distance like mosquitoes.

For old times' sake, Petar and I argued about politics over platefuls of white cheese and ripe tomatoes. Simon would join in, angry at the rise of Milosevic's take on Serbian nationalism, logical and sharp, and then I'd slowly switch off, alert to the sound but not the sense of their discussion. When two men took opposing standpoints and I could no longer play devil's advocate, I tended to feel I had nothing to contribute. I never seemed to have an opinion, and somehow always managed to see both points of view.

It might not have seemed so in Belgrade, but in Kosovo you could already smell the impending war. The smell of hot metal, sweet blood and male sweat seemed to hang in the air. In fact, when the war finally came and thousands of Serbian men scattered across the globe, preferring exile to the draft, Petar put on his uniform. He was an old-fashioned man of duty, after all, noble Bezukhov, the kind who gets used by every regime in the world and rarely gets any reward.

Simon and I took a late-night flight back to Belgrade, accompanied by a scattering of communist politicians on their way to more of the countless meetings which presaged the collapse of Yugoslavia. Petar stayed on in Macedonia. The little Yalta I engineered failed to bear fruit. They were both sensitive and stubborn, and neither was likely to change his mind. The Englishman – like a frustrated district commissioner – wanted to put the world to rights; the Serb felt his grievance too deeply to be able to be philosophical about it. We were talking about his land after all. Besides, the Englishman got the girl, and that did not necessarily make things any easier.

An almost empty plane flew low above the mountains in near-total darkness. There were villages below, lit only by the stars. When we began to descend towards Belgrade, which shimmered like a small heap of crushed ice above its two rivers, I was glad that this holiday was over.

———

The Yugoslavia I grew up in, like other socialist countries which grew up out of patriarchal, peasant societies, was a strange mixture of liberalism and restriction. In the world of work, the society I knew was already post-feminist in some ways. We grew up thinking that as far as our career choices were concerned, our gender was pretty much irrelevant. At school and at work, feminism seemed neither urgent nor entirely necessary: it was a Western indulgence, intellectually challenging but alien to our ways of thinking.

At home, however, matters were different. We had more freedoms than our mothers would have had but still lived in tightly knit, closely observed neighbourhoods. Controls were not necessarily imposed by parents, many of whom were pretty open-minded, but came from large extended families and – up to a point – the entire street you lived on. Everyone knew when you went out and when you came back. If anyone came to your door when you were not at home, neighbours would offer to take messages and invite complete strangers to await your return in their front parlour.

In matters sexual, boys were allowed as much freedom as they could get, but girls were supervised. You were not expected to have a boyfriend before you were sixteen, and by boyfriend I mean someone to go to the cinema with -- a hand to hold in the flickering darkness. While our school dances and birthday parties tingled with the charge of barely repressed sexuality, quite a few of my friends still debated whether or not one should be a virgin when one married. I was, as ever, a creature of contradiction. I occasionally dreamed of a virgin-white wedding, but I also wanted a string of lovers like a long necklace of pearls. The existence of such a dilemma and the sense of the erosion of the traditional it implies, coupled with the knowledge that in one way or another, whether or not you wanted it, you would marry, reflects the country of my adolescence. It was like the beginning of sexual intercourse in 1963, over and over again, for ever.

Nonetheless, Yugoslavia was certainly not a place of prohibition or arranged marriages, like many countries further east, but simply of increased control. One was 'allowed' one or two serious relationships before one settled down (three would be pushing your luck), and any number of suitors; in fact, the more the merrier. Suitors prone to grand gestures were the joy of every neighbourhood, and I had no shortage of those. One of these young men, a theology student, once built a snowman below my window overnight, so tall that its coal eyes peeked above the window sill of my first-floor bedroom when I opened the shutters in the morning. Another, a descendant of a Russian émigré family, once turned up in my street with a gypsy band singing '*Ochi chorniye*', 'Dark Eyes', in broken Russian with heavy Romany accents. The bandmaster was given a sheet of paper with a poem by Rimbaud, in French, yet spelled out in large Cyrillic letters, to read at my garden gate. Neighbourhood grannies would look at me walking down the road with the trained eyes of race-horse breeders, and say to each other, loudly, to tease me, 'Look at the daughter of Milos the Montenegrin, a wild filly. It will take a special man to tame her.' I studied Homer in central Belgrade, but in this former village on the outskirts of the city, I could still occasionally enter his world.

Our sex lives were controlled by the fear of pregnancy and the even greater fear of abortion, the trusty stand-by of socialist birth control. Harrowing stories of abortions gone wrong, of overworked, unsympathetic doctors and of young women's futures devastated by the wrong turn of a curettage knife were the stuff of everyday gossip. In my grandmother's day, there were two other options for a pregnant girl (three, if you counted suicide): a shotgun wedding or a cupful of caustic soda thrown in the face of the careless man. There were still a few shotgun weddings around in the late seventies, but caustic soda was not easily come by.

I knew a number of young couples forced to 'do the right thing' by bringing up a crying baby in their parents' flat, without any hope of ever affording their own place. Belgrade was a town of almost two million people and yet it somehow seemed that everyone knew everything about everyone else. Every taxi to hospital was observed and enquired about, every heartbreak carefully dissected and filed away for future reference.

It was strange, or perhaps not so strange, that such a neighbourly, tightly controlled society, which seemed to me one of the safest places in Europe, could erupt into an explosion of violence, of rapes and slaughter fuelled by rivers of drink and drugs. Even stranger that the old neighbourliness could continue to exist side by side with horrors such as refrigerated vans full of corpses dumped into the Danube; camps in which people were herded like animals; and columns of refugees stretching for miles heading for Belgrade, sometimes on tractors driven by seven-year-old boys with bricks tied to their feet because they couldn't reach the accelerator. Was it that our seemingly praiseworthy emphasis on the family reinforced our tribal identities and undercut our allegiance to wider society, so that we knew only how to defend our own? Strangest of all is

146

that, once this nightmarish version of Mardi Gras was over, so many of the old prohibitions simply slotted back into place.

———

Tomislav was an unexceptional student of civil engineering and a gifted photographer who had been one of my circle of friends since I was a teenager. Apart from coming from an almost identical family background, we had relatively little in common, but I wouldn't let that spoil the beautiful picture. I seemed to have loved the idea of Tomislav much more than I ever loved Tomislav himself. We went on a skiing holiday in Montenegro with a group of friends, about a year after I left Petar. One evening, while he and I were trying to defrost the water pipes in his family chalet by lighting a small fire in the garage, the basic chemistry of our day-to-day communication changed. Tomislav became my boyfriend with a capital B. As any viewer of romantic comedies will know, when something like this happens in the first fifteen minutes of a film, everyone sits waiting for a dark brooding stranger to take the bride away.

Tomislav was the God of Slalom: six foot four, with blond hair falling over his shoulders, eyes as blue as bluebells, and a sort of permanent tan that came from dividing his year between hours of skiing on the mountain slopes and hours of basketball on the riverside courts in Belgrade. I took him along to poetry readings. Among my fellow poets, he stood out in his white jeans and white shirt, like Michelangelo's *David*. I even introduced him to Andrei at one of these evenings, but started dragging him away before they could begin a conversation. Without being condescending, Andrei still found a way of making any man younger than forty-five look like a child, which was worrying, given that I was barely twenty-one. He also had a way of making me feel like a cat with a live bird in its jaws, about to drop the catch at his feet. To my relief, Tomislav seemed to confuse him. He clutched his drink, looked up towards the mane of blond hair and asked me about my plans for the summer holidays.

It was unsurprising, perhaps, that I liked the idea of two handsome, good-looking kids from the same side of the tracks making it together in the big world, writing books and building bridges. Neighbourhood grannies smiled at us benevolently. Even my mother got over Tomislav's habit of turning up on our doorstep in a pair of cropped shorts and a tattered shirt, carrying different bits of sports equipment or a camera around his neck. He was a nice boy from a nice family.

In the two summers we spent together, Tomislav and I would pack our rucksacks and get on to the railways of Europe, spending long, lazy days in Paris, Heidelberg or Lisbon, sometimes crossing the continent in a long seventy-two-hour sweep, or inching our way from Genoa to Barcelona for days on end, stopping to swim and eat watermelons on the white beaches of the Mediterranean. Very often, we'd simply slip into sleeping bags on the beach and watch the stars light up. We met friends from Belgrade in the most unexpected places – a Portuguese bar or a Swiss station café – and exchanged notes about youth hostels and train routes. At the end of the season, we rented a room in the walled town in Dubrovnik in which to see the summer out, floating between the azure waters and the skies of the Adriatic, without a care in the world.

At the confluence of the Danube and Sava rivers:
an early photograph by Simon

At some point between those two summers, I began to feel trapped by the pretty tapestry I was weaving. This feeling was starting to seem oddly familiar. I could not pinpoint anything grave, but I was dissatisfied with a myriad of small things. For example, Tomislav would take my photograph all the time, in a way which began to irritate me. I look at those photographs now and I see myself happy and at peace – eating my banana splits, swimming, rock climbing, sleeping, whatever – even though I know that this wasn't true. I was restless, eager not to make this my life, wishing to try other things and other people. I'd convinced myself that I was the mistress of seduction, but was increasingly bothered by the fact that I did not seem to know how to be seduced myself. And, more than anything else, I began to want to be seduced. 'You think too much,' said my younger sister wisely. I dreamed of losing my head.

———

It was strange and quite unexpected, for many different reasons, that I finally shared my life with an Englishman and by sharing it became, almost, English. Almost – in this context – is a word I am happy with, for I love the sense of being 'foreign but not quite'. I love the opportunity of reinventing myself every morning. I even love writing in a foreign language, although –

after twenty years in this country – I still can't quite control my English. Like a fast new car, it takes wide swings around unfamiliar corners and leaves me vulnerable but exhilarated.

Nonetheless, for whatever reason, I have fewer inhibitions in English – perhaps because for me it doesn't yet carry subcutaneous layers of pain. In fact, I sense – however irrational this may seem – that the I who speaks English is a very subtly different person from the I who speaks Serbian and the I who speaks French. That, perhaps, has something to do with the old chameleon tricks or the nature of the language itself. At any rate, the English speaker is a bit more blunt and a bit more direct than the other two. She is and isn't myself. She takes risks and admits to loss.

In theory, I didn't much like the idea of Britain sight unseen. All those years of Francofolly and the fact that my knowledge of these islands was based mainly on fiction had combined to make it seem a vaguely forbidding place. Beyond the white cliffs of Dover sat a rainy plateau populated, in my adolescent imagination, by depressing creatures from Hardy, Dickens, Gissing and Orwell. This is the kind of reading that my socialist educators deemed useful in exposing the reality of late capitalism.

In practice, I felt at home here from the very first day.

That is not to say that I don't feel homesick for Belgrade, for its cosy domesticity and its fragments of hard-to-find beauty. During the years of the Yugoslav wars, I often saw my native city on the news. As I watched its familiar shapes recorded through the infrared camera lens – the bomber-pilot's-eye view – I often ached with longing to be there. The outlines of the hills, rising from the murky confluence of the Sava and the Danube, were as well known to me as the curves of my own body. It might not be an accident that the two were wounded and disfigured so soon after each other.

In the summer of 1984, the Orwell year, I spent a month studying Bulgarian at the Karl Marx Institute of the University of Sofia. I rarely travelled eastwards in those days, where all there was to see seemed to be more of the same thing. I was doing some research on Byzantine prayers for my final dissertation at Belgrade University, and signing up for a Bulgarian language course, all expenses paid by the communist government of Bulgaria, was a way of getting me into the rich manuscript collections and archives of Sofia. I knew that communist propaganda would be offered in large dollops, and I didn't mind hearing some to earn my keep. I was in no danger of being reconverted.

Sofia was like the Belgrade of my early childhood, a smaller, cosier town, with fewer cars and fewer and emptier shops. Although I was there for the first time, nothing appeared to be really new. To the native speaker of Serbian, the language and the alphabet hid no secrets. The features and the physiques of Bulgarians were barely different from those of Yugoslavs, and even the food was the same. I felt almost at home, but for that noticeable difference in atmosphere which I associated with being behind the Iron Curtain, in the Eastern Bloc proper. The volume was turned down by a few notches and the lights dimmed.

My schedules were full. We had meal coupons which we were supposed to exchange in particular student canteens, and concerts, folk dances and theatre performances we were supposed to attend almost every evening. We were clearly not supposed to wander too far off the programme. Still, I did not really mind this. I'd steal a few hours in churches and museums, and after about a week I had a feeling that I'd known Sofia all my life. The feeling was compounded by the way that I seemed to keep running into people who knew me. I once popped into a post office at the other end of town, only to be stopped by a stocky young man who asked me if I'd lost my way. For some reason, he knew exactly who I was and where I was studying.

I loved the sombre Soviet atmosphere of the Karl Marx Institute. Our orderly mornings were split evenly between language lessons and history lectures explaining the glories of Bulgaria. There was a lot in those lectures that might have been challenged. The Serbs shared a great deal of history with the Bulgarians, and 'shared' was, more often than not, a euphemism for a complicated and sometimes fractious tangle. I was aware of different points of view but I never queried anything. It didn't seem courteous to my hosts, and they were nothing if not hospitable.

———

My month in Bulgaria was marked by some gloriously incongruous moments. There was, for example, a foreigners' disco at the students' hall of residence, which was obviously *the* place to see and be seen in Sofia. Every evening, it reverberated with the latest Western hits and young things turned and twisted under a complicated light show. Then there were cocktail parties and receptions for young foreign scholars, with a seemingly endless series of toasts to international friendship proposed by illustrious Bulgarian academics.

One of these cocktail parties ended with a secret ballot in what was effectively a beauty contest. You participated simply by being present, and I came third, some ten votes behind a striking Kazakh girl called Leila and a tomboyish Australian blonde. I still remember Kazashka's exotic face, and her elegant, slim body, which looked glorious even in unflattering Soviet clothes. Somewhere among my papers in Belgrade I keep a diploma which congratulates me on being 'Miss Bulgarian Summer School 1984: Second Runner Up', my trophy from the land behind the looking glass.

What 'Miss Bulgarian Summer School...' doesn't quite know how to explain is the fact that that summer in Sofia she finally managed to lose her head. What a fantastic, dizzying feeling that was! It began the evening I arrived, while I was checking into my spartan room in the student hall of residence optimistically named Spring Quarters. Sitting just outside my room, there was this amazing young thing. His long body was sprawled across an armchair. He was wearing a blue cotton shirt in the most surreal print imaginable, a pair of green agricultural labourer's trousers and tennis shoes. Behind a pair of unusual gold-and-leather-rimmed glasses glinted a pair of green eyes. His hair was

155

reddish-brown, and his skin hinted at a freckled childhood. His name was Simon.

He was obviously English, as English as the running team in *Chariots of Fire*, as English as Sebastian Flyte and the moustachioed First World War officers in my grandfather's albums of the Salonika campaign. Indeed, before long I found out that his grandfather had been just such an officer, fighting the Bulgarians alongside my forebears. He was the kind of Englishman that I spent much of my English literature courses taking apart and yet had never met before. His Englishness was fascinating, but it wasn't quite what seduced me. Rather, it was the fact that he was both strange and different and yet entirely familiar at the same time, like a long-lost twin. Coming from opposite ends of the continent, we had somehow managed to acquire the same tastes in books, films and music, and we were drawn to the same kind of places. There was no need to be chameleon-like at all. I sensed that he could be dark and difficult and broody, but he made jokes which still make me laugh after twenty years.

If there was a difference between us, it was that I was intense and openly ambitious, while he affected incredulous ignorance as I went about giving mini-lectures on anything under the sun, particularly if it could be interpreted from a post-structuralist point of view. His amateurishness was a very English affectation, just as my earnestness was a very Central European one. We both earned our Firsts soon after that Bulgarian summer: I as though anything else was out of the question, Simon as though it was an afterthought.

Between Sofia and our wedding day, we had eighteen months of Bavarian rendezvous, simply because Bavaria happened to be approximately halfway between London and Belgrade. The names of Munich underground stations still echo in my head like the most erotic of poems. Allowing yourself to be seduced turned out to be much more exciting than seducing. For one thing, you never knew what was going to happen next. I was ready to follow the boy to the end of the world, to England itself if need be.

6

GOD AND BOOKS

When a major misfortune overtakes us, people sometimes assume that – if it offers nothing else in return for the anguish – it might bring some kind of deeper spiritual insight. Suffering makes us better people – or so they say; it enables us to exhibit bravery; it makes us stronger; it brings us closer to God. We use such words of comfort because we have difficulty in accepting that suffering may come without any compensation and we create elaborate narratives of redemption around the pointlessness of pain. I can report nothing of this kind. I didn't learn anything, other than just how much pain I can take. While my cancer was attacked by poison, sword and fire, like a medieval beast, I didn't fear death. If one creates life, one doesn't just abandon the scene when the going gets tough. In a very unexpected way, the desire to be healed turned out to be about motherhood.

I continued to set the alarm clock for seven just in case I overslept, but I never did. I worked, I looked after my son and I kept the house clean. I prepared food even when the thought of eating made my stomach turn. I went from room to room with a red plastic bowl, always ready to throw up cleanly. I left handfuls of hair on the carpet, like a moulting dog. My skull emerged white and smoother than an ostrich egg. My little boy caressed my bald crown and said, 'Mummy, you look like a hatchling.' I felt younger and more vulnerable than him.

When I should have been resting, I wasted time in bookshops as though there was no tomorrow, or, judging by the extraordinary quantities of books I kept buying, as if there was a superabundance of tomorrows. I wasn't really reading anything. I sniffed the fresh smell of print and caressed unbroken spines. I indulged in macabre calculations. If I had a year to live, then, at four books a month, there was enough time to read forty-eight books; five years – 240; fifty years – 2,400. That finally offered some consolation: even without cancer, I could hardly expect to be alive fifty years from now, and yet 2,400 books seemed barely satisfactory. I already possessed 2,000 books I hadn't read, and was acquiring more each day. I was also devoting my hours to writing, which seemed a waste of precious time. I resolved to write less and read more. Reader, you are witness to my resolution.

After the first operation, I was told that I had clean, wide margins, like the books I enjoy most. I was given the odds on surviving five years, and they seemed very good, even though I couldn't really deal with odds. I am temperamentally inclined to believe that one in a thousand is somehow more likely to happen than nine out of ten.

My mother visits my father on leave, 1959

God never spoke to me. It might be that my particular pain did not really stand out in the white noise emanating from the planet like steam from a boiling pot. I certainly wasn't unwilling to get in touch. I lingered in the semi-darkness of churches just before evensong, listening out for the thin, silvery rattle of incense burners. I said prayers in English, Serbian and sometimes even in Greek. (This last sounded most likely to get through, perhaps because I understood so little of it.) It felt a bit like praying for a favourable exam result when you'd already submitted the script: comforting but useless. It might simply be that I could never be sufficiently humble. Yellow-faced and radiation-sick, Daldilocks remained her obstinate self.

Nonetheless, only bookshops and churches gave me the feeling that anything might happen. I didn't really believe in God as much as I believed in books, but I loved the sights and sounds of religion. The Byzantine chant of my ancestral Orthodoxy, curtains of incense and black-clad monks with beards untouched by razors, flocking like ravens on snow-covered forecourts; Anglican cathedrals in which stone seemed as light as ice cream; the sublime, darkened beauty of London's Tractarian churches; the Baroque waxworks of ripe Catholicism – as far as I was concerned, they all provided a vision of humanity at its most endearingly hopeful. And London was the

New Jerusalem: there was no religion in the world which didn't have a meeting house in one of its suburban terraces. Being ill in the British capital at the beginning of the twenty-first century was a bit like being a leper in the Holy Land in AD 33: there was never a shortage of volunteers to wash one's feet.

I went to synagogues and mosques. On balance, I preferred domes to arches: building a sphere, a woman's breast, seemed as close as both God and humanity ever came to perfection. Looking at the webs of unfamiliar script, I realized that the vocabulary of my own, non-existent faith was so bound up in the story of Jesus that I couldn't get him out of my mind. I said God and, pop, up came the long bearded face. Although I might have tried to undo such conditioning, it seemed hardly worth the effort. Since it was unlikely that I was ever going to believe, I might as well remain a Serbian Orthodox agnostic. Other religions appealed as stories, Christianity as a storybook with pictures.

If I believed anything, it was that – as the novelist Danilo Kis once said – reading many books could never be as dangerous as reading just one. My literary hoards offered a sense of peace that no single volume has ever been able to provide on its own, but I did begin to wonder what was behind my obsessive book buying. In my family history, building a library has always

162

seemed a bad idea. Books vanished when your house was hit by a bomb or torched, and they were what had to be left behind when you moved abroad. In difficult times, a diamond ring could always be exchanged for a pot of goose fat in one of the villages surrounding Belgrade. All a book can do is burn.

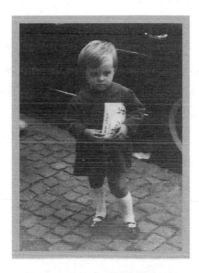

Two years old, with my favourite book

I am a compulsive reader. Quality doesn't really come into this. On crowded underground trains, when there is no room to open a book, I will read safety warnings and advertisements, breaking the lines in different places to create a poem. Put me into a bare hotel room and I'll go through the phone directories imagining local lives, the way other people may flick through satellite TV channels. On those occasions when I said 'yes' to proposals I'd never intended to accept and was then duty-bound to oblige, it happened because I was reading while pretending to listen. If I travelled anywhere, the safe bet is that I carried more books than clothes, fearing that I might run out of things to read. Even then, I went straight to the airport bookshop to buy more.

Feverishly starting a new volume, reading to page sixty or thereabouts, and then moving on to the next one, so that I always had at least six or seven books on the go, has always been my particular vice. Books gathered by my pillow, in my desk drawers, in bags abandoned at the bottom of my wardrobe, like sweet wrappers in a child's pocket. The space under my bed was known in my family as the Library of Congress. If I woke up in the middle of the night, I'd reach down there and pull out a book to continue to read from where I last left it, the place marked by a bus ticket from Tel Aviv to Acre dated 1988 or a letter I began writing seven years ago. My memories of places became inseparable from the books I first read while visiting them. Sometimes the connections made geographic sense – like discovering André Aciman's *Out of Egypt* in Alexandria – sometimes not at all. I read Kiš's *Early Sorrows* while staying with a

retired colonel in Peshawar, and the book still colours my recol-
lections of the North-West Frontier Province with Central
European melancholy.

My fondest memories from abroad are those of standing in
bookshops, inhaling the familiar smell of leather, paper and
fresh print. On one of my earliest visits to England, I discovered
paradise in the shadows of St Paul's Cathedral. It was a
bookshop where books could be had for free if you plausibly
impersonated a visitor from behind the Iron Curtain. I am not
sure which democracy-loving, communist-hating organization
funded the enterprise. The little shop was well stocked with the
works of dissident East European authors and right-wing
economic theory. The former enthralled for hours. Every book
ever banned in the East seemed to be there, from the grand-
daddy of dissidents, my Montenegrin compatriot Milovan Djilas,
to the Bulgarian Georgi Markov, who was murdered with a stab
from a poisoned umbrella tip on London's Waterloo Bridge.
Elegant novels written by Czech rubbish collectors stood next to
Albanian essayists, and imprisoned Romanian poets vied for
shelf space with Lithuanian philosophers. When you chose your
books, an elderly bookseller (or book-giver) produced a form

which required your signature and address. For some unaccountable reason, I gave a Bulgarian name, feeling, perhaps, that the provenance was more suitable for a recipient of such literary gifts. It didn't seem like the sort of place where anyone would ask you to produce your documents: that would be too much like home. By the time I settled in London, my paradise had gone.

In my second year at Belgrade University I decided to become a palaeographer. I gave up work as a youth radio presenter in order to join a course in Byzantine Greek. My mother was distraught. My bright media future was evaporating before her eyes, giving way to musty old libraries and mustier salaries. Working with old manuscripts did not seem at all glamorous to her. She thought I was too good-looking to be a palaeographer. Granny was worried that I might catch bubonic plague from a bug dormant in some twelfth-century manuscript which I happened to open for the first time since its scribe collapsed, hands covered in horrible, pus-filled fistulas, clutching his quill pen. Only my father saw some consolation in the fact that it was the kind of work which was unlikely to lead to imprisonment. There seemed to be nothing remotely political in transcribing thousand-year-old prayers, whereas as a media star I was likely to shoot my mouth off sooner or later.

My medieval literature tutor, an erudite Byzantine scholar who was quietly anti-communist and unapologetically elitist in his ideas of higher education, took much of both the credit and the blame for this sudden conversion. He guided me and Irena, a fellow literature student and one of my closest friends, to every manuscript collection in Belgrade, there to discover the secrets of book-copying. Irena was a gentle, blonde Montenegrin girl who reminded everyone of Mariel Hemingway in Woody Allen's film *Manhattan*, and our tutor – in his tweed jackets, turtle-neck jumpers and round spectacles – was most comfortingly donnish. Of the three, I was the one who was least like a palaeographer. I could never decide whether to dress like the businesswoman of the year, a lover of Jean-Paul Sartre or a punk.

The archives, with their old bookcases and desks, provided a refuge from an increasingly impoverished, polluted city. Belgrade was becoming like Cairo without the pyramids, or Erzerum with traffic jams and queues. The quiet world of faith inscribed in red initials and black continuous script seemed to provide the best sanctuary I could find. I might not be able to believe in God myself, but I was awed by the belief I witnessed. Irena and I looked at textual variants and transmission errors, we measured column widths, counted accents and breathings, and tabulated the family trees of manuscripts, feeling frighteningly, wonderfully grown up. I am not sure if any English undergraduate would be allowed to lay his or her hands on such treasures. Irena is still a gifted palaeographer. I obviously had no staying power. My mother was right: I was not cut out for archival work. I wanted to be quiet and at peace, but I was one of those children who are always, and in spite of their better judgement, driven to giggles by too much silence.

In fact, while it was highly unlikely that a palaeographer would end up in prison or without a job, as has been known to happen to the critics of contemporary literature, my father was wrong in thinking that the vellum-bound world was apolitical. You could say, for example, that a manuscript was 'probably Bulgarian' or 'possibly twelfth-century', and cause an international dispute of major proportions. In the Balkans, there has always been an unspoken competition as to who was the first to be civilized as well as to who was the most civilized. Manuscripts provided forensic evidence. Given that medieval monks left relatively few clues pointing to their chosen national identity, one sometimes felt a bit like a Mormon, rechristening one's ancestors. Certainly, whether Methodius the Hypothetical was a Bulgarian, a Serb or quite possibly Greek seemed so much more important than whether T. S. Eliot was British or American. My on-the-one-hand-and-then-on-the-other attitude was never going to be an asset. As a palaeographer, you were expected to have an opinion, and I've never had an unqualified opinion in my life, at least not until I was forty one.

—

I gave a lecture on Danilo Kis's novel *A Tomb for Boris Davidovich* in London in the late eighties. Together with quite a few of my compatriots, I was a teeny-weeny bit in love with Danilo, who was a tall, slim, Jewish-Hungarian-Montenegrin Byron. I remember seeing him walk along Belgrade's Knez Mihajlova Street through a thick curtain of snow, with snowflakes melting in his dark curls. A woman called out his name and he responded in a deep, smoky voice. I remained smitten for three weeks at least: I was barely fourteen and hadn't yet read any of his books.

As I explained Kis's post-national credentials, a Hungarian woman in the audience stood up to ask me whether I thought Danilo was in fact a Hungarian Jew or a Jewish Hungarian. 'You and I know what the difference means,' she suggested conspiratorially. Danilo called himself 'the last Yugoslav' but I wasn't sure if that really meant anything to him. At that stage he was already dying in his Parisian exile, and a couple of years later I put a pebble on his grave. I often described myself as Yugoslav simply because I kept forgetting that the country did not exist any more. I felt utterly defeated.

———

When I gave up palaeography, I decided to try my hand at deconstruction. I read every volume on post-structuralism I could put my hands on in Belgrade – not that many, in those days – and started penning book reviews neither of my parents could make any sense of. Soon enough, I became editor of the student literary magazine *Znak*, 'The Sign'. It was one of the most coveted positions a young literary thing could have. The budget was considerable and there was no pressure to sell, which, curiously, often produced better results than more financially minded publishing ventures. I began to describe myself as a fellow-traveller of the postmodernist school.

In the eighties, the debate between the 'realists' and the 'postmodernists' had suddenly become very public and very bitter. Mostly middle-aged and mostly men, the realists thought that an author should be engaged or, as they put it, 'rise up to the challenges of their society'. In those days, this meant being a nationalist, or – as the realists would have it – 'patriotic'. The postmodernists were mainly young and smart, and responded to the 'challenges of the society' by writing fiction which had very little to do with anything, and was so sophisticated it hurt. I tried to publish as much of their work as possible in my two years at the helm of *Znak*. In fact, I was probably never as happy as when going to our printers in New Belgrade with my hands full of galley proofs of experimental prose. I took unnecessarily long routes and stopped to chat to everyone.

I had a little office at the university, which became the meeting place of the smart set, or so I fancied. I spent my nights translating chunks of deconstructionist philosophy, smoking out of my bedroom window, nurturing my conceits and weighing my career options. Many of my postmodernist brethren were ending up in America. I imagined a professorship at Columbia (good location, good university), but Yale seemed to be the place where deconstruction was happening. I wasn't so sure about New Haven, but decided that – if the package Yale offered was good – I'd reluctantly have to move out to the sticks. The wielding of literary power – however small – was obviously corrupting.

For students of literature such as myself, who thought themselves men and women of letters, Belgrade was in many ways a
sort of down-at-heel Elysium. It might be true that there are
more literary events in London in any given week than in a
whole year of book publishing in Serbia, but the illusion that
you could do everything and get everywhere had tremendous
compensations. From the protest meetings at the Writers' Union
to the decadent, avant-garde happenings at the Students'
Cultural Centre, our little duffel-coated coterie of literary critics
in their early twenties seemed omnipresent. We asked questions
and collected signatures, we booed and applauded across the
town. We hung on the tails of famous literary visitors to the
capital, in the illusion that we were – in the wider scheme of
things – somehow part of the world into which people like
Czeslaw Milosz, Joseph Brodsky, Allen Ginsberg and John
Updike casually dropped. I was star-struck by writers. I built up
a collection of books with personal dedications from the great
and the good of the writing world, many of whom weren't sure
whether they were in Belgrade, Bucharest or Budapest.

I have a file of poems with rhymes for Vesna in a number of
languages, written amid the bibulous aftermaths of the many

readings I attended. Being, as my mother insisted, a good-looking girl, as well as the editor of Belgrade's most avant-garde literary journal (or so I kept telling anyone who cared to listen, and many did), I even received marriage proposals, one of which was delivered in Welsh, by a grey-haired poet kneeling in the lobby of the Excelsior Hotel in Belgrade. I am not sure if it was the thought of being in Eastern Europe which brought out the romantic (or opportunistic) streak in visiting Western writers. I was still too naive to enquire whether a hand offered in marriage was a euphemism for anything else. That naivety was also perhaps what protected me from actually finding out.

———

On occasion, I acted as an interpreter from French for the Writers' Union. I soon realized that the thrill of being in the East, where books mattered more than life itself, was what many of our literary visitors found exciting about the idea of coming to Belgrade. They always wanted to know about banned authors and banned books, about poets imprisoned and tortured for their verse. I loved the idea of dangerous books myself, but it often seemed that most of Yugoslavia's banned authors were nationalists, and that didn't seem romantic at all.

It seemed, in a way, disappointing that we were not more like Russia used to be in the thirties, or earlier. One French poet enthused over my alleged 'striking resemblance' to Tatiana from Pushkin's *Eugene Onegin*. 'TatiaNA,' he called across the lobby when I came to pick him up from his hotel for his morning meetings, sweetly emphasizing the last syllable. 'TatiaNA', he sang in the official limousine all the way to the state dairy in Panchevo, at the other side of the Danube, a visit to which was organized by some clever-clogs bureaucrat in the town hall. 'Don't worry, TatiaNA,' he whispered as I struggled in my efforts to convey comparative data related to the milk production of Holstein-Friesians and Brown Swiss cows into French. 'Just tell me sweet nothings, if you prefer. No one will ever know.'

When I came to live in London in 1986, it took me seven months to find a job. I might have got one sooner had I not – in a fit of newcomer's stubbornness – restricted myself to replying to the few job ads published in the *Times Literary Supplement* and the *London Review of Books*. Eventually, an Anglo-Czech science-fiction writer, who earned his living by working for a Cambridge publisher in an office high in one of the turrets of the Natural History Museum in South Kensington, was sufficiently intrigued

174

by my unconventional CV to want to interview me. Soon afterwards I became an editor, but I edited nothing. I spent most of my time drawing up production grids for a microfiche collection of books about plants and insects, a job for which the one essential qualification was an ability to count to forty-nine, the number of frames on the microfiche.

I spent my days in a bizarre mimicry of reading. I turned the pages of literally thousands of books, and plotted out the microfiche frames, which I then passed on to an English history graduate who was the 'photography editor'. From this angle, British publishing seemed to be full of people whose job titles were far too grand for what they actually did, as if to compensate for salaries which would barely keep one afloat in Kishinev.

For the first time in my life, I worked with books which contained nothing I was remotely interested in. Not being English, I was left pretty cold by botany and entomology. I was a town girl, uninterested in plant and insect life; in my native Serbian, I knew the names of hundreds of species, purely for poetic purposes, but when it came to recognizing any, I am afraid that identifying the most basic – a butterfly, an oak or a rose – was as far as my expertise went.

Nonetheless, I was surrounded by some of the most beautiful books I've ever seen. Just being in a library made me happy: it was a world whose driving forces and divisions of labour were as familiar to me as a beehive is to a bee. Librarians pulled out catalogue drawers crammed tight with index cards; scientists waited for large volumes to be delivered to ornate, numbered desks. From my little cubbyhole, high under one of the neo-Gothic arches of the museum, I observed them going about their business and entertained myself by inventing elaborate stories of plant and insect gathering in Belize or the Caucasus. One day, I was a writer in exile, recently escaped from East Berlin or Kaliningrad with a 100,000-word masterpiece, another – a princess in her castle.

I had a chatelaine of keys which took me through under-ground corridors full of stuffed animals, bizarre specimens in formaldehyde and all kinds of other exhibits that were no longer appropriate for show, to cellars and then up to turrets full of books. I occasionally spoke to an entomologist with an interest in Russian coleoptera, who told me that many of his colleagues in the museum believed I was Russian because I once helped him translate a Russian index card. There was also an occasion when some botanists invited me to meet a 'compatriot of mine', a visiting professor from Budapest, and didn't seem at all puzzled when we started conversing in French. I didn't help matters by always explaining my nationality in the most complicated way possible. My museum security pass gave 'Belgravia' as my place of birth.

Two years into my first job, I barely knew anyone in the publishing firm for which I worked. I met the proprietor, a charming baronet, once, for about five minutes. Cyril, my Czech interviewer, left more or less the moment I proved I could be relied on to count to forty-nine. He warned me that the job would leave me bored out of my wits. This would have been daunting for some people, but I loved the prospect of boredom. Growing up in Eastern Europe was a powerful vaccine. I had gone through eighteen years of socialist education, learning when to say yes and when to keep quiet, in preparation for a job in which I'd be underpaid and under-employed. Where I come from, such jobs – usually in very nice places – were often described as 'ideal for women'.

———

I continued to meet Cyril from time to time, mainly in pubs around South Kensington, where we would talk about East European science fiction and world music, his pet subjects. He was now indexing place-names for an expensive edition of the Domesday Book which was being prepared by another small publisher. He explained to me that the Domesday Book was a glorified eleventh-century tax return rather than, as I thought, a book of apocalyptic prophecy. Cyril remembered that I knew some Latin and could read *scripta continua* and offered me a job in an office in a former dairy behind Kensington Square. I rang Cambridge and told my boss that I had been 'head-hunted': a fine display of Thatcherite vocabulary, which was then just beginning to filter through to the gentle world of independent publishing.

Cyril and I – a Czech and a Serb – now spent hours over huge maps of English counties, plotting the exact locations of salt-pans, forests and demesnes in the eleventh century and finding them on large Ordnance Survey maps. England still seemed like an enormous jigsaw puzzle to me. While I got to know individual counties down to the smallest hamlet, I often had no idea where they stood in relation to each other. I loved the weird poetry of English place-names. I'd repeat strange little mantras – 'Chester-le-Street, Ashby de la Launde, Ashby de la Zouch, Weston-super-Mare' – as though I was bringing the country of my marriage into being.

As the 'place-name editor', I often dealt with calls from prospective buyers, who invariably wanted to ensure that their house or their village was mentioned in the Domesday Book before they parted with their money. On hearing a foreign female, many asked to speak to 'my boss', so I usually transferred the calls to our marketing director, Lady Henrietta. There was no point in alienating customers by trying to prove something. Slim and elegant, with a singsong plummy voice, Lady Henrietta seemed to me a born saleswoman. I could sometimes hear her saying to one of the people to whom I'd spoken that I was 'frighteningly clever', which always pleased me. There were many more English people in London in those days, and foreigners tended to fall into one of two categories: they were either fiendishly clever, spoke ten languages fluently and knew everything, or they had to be taught how to hold a fork and run water from a tap. I was glad to find myself in the first category.

Eventually, I progressed beyond place-names, to some proper copy-editing. The Domesday Book was an endless variation on the 'Ethelred the Lecher owns two pigs and a copse in Lower Turnpike' theme, so there was not much to be brainy about. I now sat at a desk in the corner of a large office which belonged to Robert, the editorial director, art historian, son of an earl and one of the most terrific raconteurs I've come across. I could listen for hours to his stories, few of which had anything to do with the Domesday Book. In the sixties, the publisher I worked for had produced brave, adventurous books illustrated by some of the most avant-garde artists of the day, instead of the good-looking volumes in green and gold – the publishing equivalent of

National Trust soap bars – which we were now putting out. I had a feeling, one which I often had in England, that I had arrived somewhere just after the party was over, and that the best thing to do was have one last drink and hear how it all went. No one was better suited to that than Robert.

Our office was like a room in an eccentric museum. Pieces of Robert's eclectic collection of artworks were literally everywhere: an Aboriginal feather cloak, a threadbare kilim, sculpture from India and psychedelic prints from the sixties, came together in a fascinating mess. In the early afternoon, Robert and I often drank wine from milky Roman glasses which, he would say, may or may not have been touched by Jesus. He would sometimes nod off and leave me to edit my ploughs and furlongs to the gentle sound of snoring. We were paid a pittance, but even so there was never enough money to keep us all going. In Moscow, we might have gone on for several decades, but here the writing was clearly on the wall. While it lasted, it was England as I liked it best.

———

In the years of horror brought on by the interminable war in my homeland, I retreated to the world of reading lists, seminar discussions and essay deadlines, in which I always felt safe and at home, first as a student and then as a teacher. The former polytechnic, one of Britain's newest generation of universities, of which I finally became part, may not have turned out to be quite the glamorous oasis of electrifying lectures in elegant wood-panelled halls I had envisaged while furtively smoking fragrant Herzegovina cigarettes out of the window of my Zharkovo bedroom, but there were always just enough students who cared about books to make me feel that I was in the right place after all. And once every two or three years, there was one whose passion was such that it carried me along. I understood, for the first time, that what I thought of as Andrei's gift to me – those hours of apprenticeship which made me feel privileged to be his student – might just as easily have been my gift to him.

There were many moments in which my sense of homecoming was less than poetic. One April day a couple of years ago, I escaped early from a meeting which was stumbling into its fourth hour and had only just reached item nine out of the seventeen points on the agenda. In the art of the long meeting, British university workers easily outdid anything I'd encountered in my socialist upbringing. The sessions were often longer than the communist plenaries, the acronyms just as plentiful, the put-downs just as complicatedly veiled in oblique metaphor, the passions just as high, even if the stakes were often infinitesimal.

The Yugoslavs and the Warsaw Pacters were at least allowed drink and cigarettes in their meetings; my colleagues and I were slowly boring each other to death over weak tea and cheap sugary biscuits, in grey classrooms where one's eye followed dark circles of chewing gum on the floor and the smell of crisps and trainers continued to linger even through the long summer vacation. In its functionality, its determined denial of beauty, the university was visually so East European that I often had to check myself when the phone rang in my office, for fear that I might answer it in Serbian.

I walked through the quiet avenues of Kingston Hill feeling guilty about the hour I'd stolen. Large villas hid behind impenetrable crowns of trees. Every now and then a car came by and its driver threw a curious glance at me. We were miles away from public transport but no one was walking here, and quite a few streets had no pavements. I had to stay either in the middle of the road or walk along the wet verges, where my feet sank into the grass with a soft, squashy sound. It felt as though the water was rising from below. I couldn't decide if it was raining or not, so I kept opening and closing my umbrella.

I was trying to guess how my life would turn out, paradoxically, just at the moment when – unknown to me – the first mutant cells may have begun to attach themselves to my milk ducts. In theory, I had a job I'd always thought I wanted, and I was good at it. In practice, I no longer felt I could get everything I pointed a finger at, which had been my secret magic. I could not work out where and when I lost that feeling. There was the decade-long, draining war, which left the country I came from destitute and friendless. Then there was the more immediate poverty around me, not nearly as devastating, but sad nonetheless. The poverty of the publishing world managed to seem romantic, whereas the bleak poverty of the university often upset me, perhaps because there were so many young witnesses to it. It seemed unfair that they couldn't have what I had had so long ago, and in a much poorer place.

My own time was increasingly thrown against the advancing waves of bureaucracy. I often sat over spreadsheets at my dining-room table late into the night, working out percentages of this and that, just like my mother used to do. Even the abbreviations I used in my reports were eerily similar to the ones with which she headed the miles of ledgers she used to produce. There was no inherent reason why my life should be any easier than hers. Nonetheless, I felt that I was betraying some kind of promise I'd given her by accepting the boredom so readily, as though both of us had somehow failed through that acceptance, for what kept her going was the illusion that her children's lives would somehow turn out to be miraculously easy.

I had believed that I could somehow dedicate my life to the beauty of the written word, but it sometimes seemed that books were no longer enough and this was really confusing. I was not made for asceticism. I hated austerity. Perhaps for the first time since I arrived in England, I began to feel claustrophobic. I was about to enter the tropic of Cancer, that twilight world from which one longs to return to ledgers and spreadsheets at midnight, indeed to anything at all which could be called simply life.

———

In the forties, in a room in the coach house which stood in the Japanese garden of Warren House, the Kingston Hill residence of Lady Paget, the Serbian novelist Milos Tsernianski wrote the second volume of *Migrations*, a haunting story of exile and loss, one of the greatest Slavonic books. The Tsernianskis could not afford to pay rent, and repaid their benefactress in kind. Milos, a former Yugoslav diplomat, used his calligraphic skills to address her party invitations and his wife, Vida, baked biscuits for Lady Paget's guests. It is terribly unfair, but I keep thinking of the couple as pets, a pair of Pekinese perhaps. I imagine Lady Paget turning towards one of her friends and saying, against the clinking of porcelain cups, 'I keep a Serbian novelist here, you know, my dear.' To his credit, Tsernianski was never a particularly grateful guest: indeed, the veiled references to his hostess in his novels are invariably ironical and bitter. He was a pet piranha rather than a pet Pekinese, biting the hand which fed him. I briefly saw myself in my own coach house at the bottom of Kingston Hill, baking biscuits and writing party invitations, although I no longer had the kind of conceit which would make me feel Tsernianski's equal without having done anything to prove it. On the other hand, I had one enormous advantage over him. I was free to come and go as I pleased. I needed to feel that freedom in my bones again if I was to survive.

Sisters on the grass

In the early thirties, my Herzegovinian grandfather was visiting Subotica, a town close to the Yugoslav border with Hungary, when he met his future Montenegrin bride. Subotica was the birthplace of James Joyce's Leopold Bloom, a confection of Habsburg neo-Baroque and Jugendstil where poplars and spires still provide the highest points on the cityscape. It is built on land so flat that it tricks the eye into seeing the earth's surface bend and slope off towards the horizon. After the Great War, hundreds of Montenegrins were settled on the farmland around Subotica, in order to firm up the new border of the kingdom of Serbs, Croats and Slovenes. They continued to yearn for the mountains well into the third generation.

Because of an administrative error, my grandmother's identity card lists Subotica as her birthplace, even though she was born 300 miles further south, in what used to be the kingdom of Montenegro. An educated, well-to-do girl from a good tribe, of which she remained fiercely proud, my grandmother might have married a Sirdar or a courtier. She had raven-black hair and deep-set eyes like sloes. The Great War left her with an invalid father, shipwrecked in the northern plains. She worked in a rope factory to support her younger siblings through school. Surrounded by Hungarian, German and Romanian workers, she picked up words from their languages and for the rest of her life spoke 'Granny', a unique Montenegrin-Central European dialect in which Ottoman and Austro-Hungarian layers of vocabulary blended into a singular concoction. No one else in the world spoke this language; her parents were too old to change their speech, her siblings too young to remember the inflections of the old country. Granny's voice was coarse with asthma – a memento from the years she spent inhaling hemp dust on the factory floor.

I sometimes ring my little sister in her important big office in Toronto and leave a message in 'Granny' on her voicemail. I adopt an asthmatic wheeze and let flow a torrent in which complaints and endearments alternate in a linguistic *macé doine*, until I run out of breath and start laughing. My grandmother's rages were biblical, her outpourings of love unmatched. Her way of speaking always seems several sizes too big for me. The telephone line which connects me to my sister's answering machine in the depths of the Canadian winter conveys a code which is more perfect than any my father in his career as a codebreaker ever deciphered. The language of my dead grandmother brings to life all our lost homelands, yet no book has ever been written in it. This is the language I lost when I chose to write books in English, a choice I affirmed when English turned out to be my son's mother tongue. When I capture the code in the language of my son, I'll burn the books and set myself free.

7

HOMESICKNESS, WAR AND RADIO

One of the games my sister and I liked to play when we were children was called 'television'. We'd put two chairs side by side at the dining-room table, sit upright and smile beatifically towards imaginary cameras as we shuffled the blank sheets of paper from which we 'read' our news bulletins. We had our *noms de plume*, or, rather, *noms de microphone*. 'Respected viewers, good evening,' my sister would begin, with the standard opening of Belgrade TV news. 'Comrade Tito visited a factory today. Over to you, Natasha.' 'Thank you, Clementine,' I'd say, carefully enunciating every syllable.

My lips were the colour of violets. Before a broadcast we 'went into make-up': early on, we played each other's make-up girls, but then, because of different approaches to aesthetics, each started doing her own. Father had a stash of marker crayons in the garage, red on one side and blue on the other, of an old-fashioned kind which needed a lick in order to write. The crayons made convincing make-up tools: blue for the eyelids, red for the cheeks, a layer of red followed by a layer of blue for the lips, and, only occasionally, a fragrant cloud of Mother's face powder to finish. My sister was fond of fake moles. I hated the way she sometimes read the news looking like a shrunken version of Madame de Pompadour, but I was in no position to choose my co-anchors at that stage. My sister was the only show in town. While she went on as cheerfully as ever, my growing hostility became apparent in my broadcasts, which I increasingly delivered through clenched teeth.

In those days, news readers on Belgrade television were not really journalists. They tended to be elegant men and women with sonorous, educated voices, selected as much for their political suitability as for their poise and reading skills. News bulletins were static affairs which followed a strict running order. No matter what was going on in the world, Comrade Tito's activities came first. Foreign news could be as bleak as you liked, but home offerings were generally cheerful and positive. Sports achievements followed news of production quotas met and surpassed and the export successes of Yugoslav industry. Contented tourists from around the world visited our coast, and Yugoslav cars raced along the roads of foreign capitals.

It was easy to produce convincing imitations of such daily litanies of success, but they made our broadcasting game repetitive. My sister and I desperately needed excitement and disasters. We occasionally tried to interview our grandmother for the programme, sensing some potential in her story, but she kept rejecting our bids. She never believed anything anyone said in the news bulletins, not even the weather reports, and was indifferent towards the idea of media stardom. Furthermore, she tended to enquire about the nationality of any person who appeared on television, and – if it was a Montenegrin – say something along the lines of, 'I knew it. You do not get much more handsome or cleverer than that.' It was only because of her that we noticed that Montenegro, not much more populous than a small British county, produced a disproportionate number of talking heads. This might have had something to do with its beautiful but barren landscape: there was little point in trying to make a go of it at home.

Granny loved agricultural programmes, boxing and Montenegrin folk-dancing – which was itself a convincing imitation of fighting. That was about it as far as television was concerned. She would stay up late watching international boxing championships and always chose her favourites according to their religion. So long as the Orthodox boys won, she was happy; unfortunately, in the world of boxing, that did not happen very often. Mother was exasperated. How could such a seemingly sweet old thing be so fond of savage entertainment and yet cheerfully talk her way through the New Year's Day concert from Vienna which was Mother's favourite TV programme? As far as Mother was concerned, Granny's Montenegrin blood was to blame for all her unladylike excesses.

On those rare occasions when our house filled with those Montenegrin cousins with whom my grandmother was still on speaking terms, and the noise of their arguments became unbearable, Mother would beckon me to the kitchen to help arrange the trays of *meze*. Closing the door behind her, she sighed in resignation. She could never accept the fact that arguing was just the way they communicated. They knew how to keep quiet when they wanted. It was not uncommon to find close relatives living under the same roof who hadn't said a word to each other for ten years because of some tiff the origins of which were long forgotten.

Mother was particularly incensed by Granny's way of dividing people into friend or foe according to their faith, or, rather, according to her perception of it. If one were to believe Granny, the whole of Asia and Africa was 'Turkish' and most of the rest of the world Catholic, and we were never quite sure which was worse. The Jews, whom she called *Chivuti*, were great, both because they continued to stand up to the 'Turks' and because communist Yugoslavia was hostile to Israel (and anything maligned by that bunch was *ipso facto* fantastic), but one couldn't quite escape the feeling that that was because she had never really met any Jews, Israeli or otherwise. One thing was certain: we Orthodox folk had to stick together! Not that, in her case, that ever stood in the way of expressing prejudice about Romanians, Bulgarians, Greeks or, in particular, her fellow Serbs. While the Serbs from the highlands were generally OK, those from the lowlands were a bunch of thieves to a man.

How all this annoyed Mother! She was too polite to argue, but she would turn towards Granny and say, 'Mother, how can you?' in a steady, even tone, using the polite form of *you*. In the thirty years they lived together, my mother preserved the formal *vi* – the Serbian second-person plural – in addressing her mother-in-law, whereas Granny was on familiar, *ti* terms with everyone, including God, with whom she argued incessantly and loudly as though he were a fellow Montenegrin. 'Why wouldn't you do this for me, God?' she prayed, sounding the word God as though it were a Christian name. 'Have I ever thrown a stone at you?'

My sister or I would raise a small, clenched fist – the imaginary microphone – towards Mother's lips, sensing a statement fit for our news bulletins. 'You should never, ever judge people by their faith,' Mother would say, making sure that Granny was within earshot, with examples of wonderful friends who were either Catholic or Muslim at the ready. The older woman shrugged her shoulders and waited for the knockout.

———

In 1992, as the long agony of Yugoslavia's dissolution gathered pace, I became the night-shift queen of the BBC World Service. I was still playing at journalism, while my little sister became the news. She worked for the Belgrade offshoot of a British charity, on whose behalf she took risks on the fringes of Balkan battlefields where she struggled to reunite children found alone in shelters and orphanages with families exiled across the continent, from Lapland to Anatolia. Because of the war, children's homes were full of kids who didn't really know whether they still had parents or not. My sister is a mother of two, and her heart broke on a daily basis. She showed me a self-portrait made by one of her wards, a clumsy sketch by a seven-year-old depicting a boy kicking a football. The leg which pointed towards the ball was a short, thin line in pencil. 'An unfinished drawing?' I asked.

'A landmine,' replied my sister. 'Thank you,' the caption read, in a shaky child's hand.

———

Just before four a.m., I glance out of my office window at the BBC towards the ink-coloured sky behind the pigeon mesh. This is the most dangerous hour for night-shift workers: lorries swerve towards lampposts, hands slip under mechanized blades, hospital patients die, bleepers emit a long, steady whine. The worst I can do is fluff during the five o'clock news bulletin: give the wrong time, a wrong date, an incorrect temperature. In rare moments of panic, when no tape seems to be in its proper place and telephone connections with stringers in distant Balkan valleys remain obstinately dead, my brain short-circuits and I start apologizing to my listeners in English. Wires cross and spark, producing a millisecond of blank space in which I begin to say *sorry* instead of *izvinite*. I emit no more than a barely audible hiss, which startles the studio manager on the other side of the heavy glass panel, before I realize the mistake and will my tired mind to think in Serbian again. As soon as the steady, incomprehensible Slavonic flow resumes, the SM settles back into his chair. The TV above his head broadcasts silent explosions and train crashes in slow motion. I try not to look at the ticker at the bottom of the screen, for fear that I might start speaking English again.

Serbian – the language of the news bulletins I read every night from the basement of Bush House, the BBC World Service's Art Deco edifice in Aldwych – is my mother tongue, but English is now both more and much less than that. It is my default language, the code in which apologies are proffered. I have written millions of words, made love thousands of times, been ill, dreamed and prayed in English. I have cooked countless meals using herbs and spices whose names do not exist in any other language in my mind, while broadcasting in what itself must be becoming something quaintly archaic: the 'RP' spoken by Belgrade's educated classes, the language which, in its own turn, both is and isn't my own tongue.

My 'real' Serbian is intoned with long, open stresses which resonate in the voices of kids playing ball in the streets of Belgrade's inner suburbs. It is peppered with corrupted English slang, with which my generation has replaced my granny's German *hoch* and my mother's French *comme il faut*: that 'hepi' which does and does not mean 'happy', the 'fensi' which means pretentious rather than just 'fancy', the 'OK' which is and isn't yes. It is usually delivered in a sort of dead-pan in which everything you say turns out to mean its exact opposite: the vocal equivalent of a Masonic handshake. Over the years in England, I have lost not only the words but also the gestures that go with it – the shrug of the shoulders for 'What can one do?', the full-stop pout for emphasis, the wave-away for those who are beyond redemption. When I do make them, the movements feel as though they belong to someone else.

The Bulgarians shake their heads from side to side for yes, and nod for no: the head gestures' meaning is the exact opposite of that further west in Europe. I remember my Bulgarian summer of 1984 – the summer in which I met Simon – as the summer when I laughed as I said no while nodding vigorously, and said yes while shaking my head as if in disbelief. Although his Bulgarian was much better than mine, my future husband wisely stuck to his English gestures. This riddled the progress of our affair with potential for misinterpretation. Not that there was ever any misunderstanding, for in the things which mattered we barely needed to speak to each other. Words are, after all, only a small part of knowing the language.

My English vocabulary was fairly extensive when I settled in Britain in 1986. My parents had spent thousands on their daughters' English classes over the years, an investment which was ultimately to take us both away from them. What I had yet to learn was the English communication code: how to distinguish the compliments from put-downs and courtesies from real invitations; how to know when I was free to laugh and when laughter would be in bad taste. Over the years, I've even learned how to punctuate my speech with those peculiarly English smiles which light the face for a brief moment and disappear as quickly as they've come. My mother tongue, meanwhile, remained firmly locked in its mid-eighties Serbo-Croat time capsule, a language which officially does not even exist any more.

———

Some months before I decided to join the World Service, I took Kosta, an old Belgrade friend who now lived in Illinois, out to lunch in a Soho restaurant. Having just come from a brief visit to Belgrade, he was full of home-grown gossip. It seemed as though everyone we knew was having affairs, divorcing and making futile bids for freedom from the middle-aged duties we were all slowly beginning to accumulate. Kosta and I laughed our way through two bottles of wine before we got to where we always get in the end, the stories which still, just about, keep us anchored in a vanished world. Deliberately avoiding any talk of the war, we were like bright orange buoys with chains almost eaten away by the salt, bobbing happily on the surface of things.

In our university days, for example, you were allowed to smoke while sitting exams, and many future literary critics anxiously availed themselves of the opportunity to calm their frayed nerves, while invigilators smoked to pass the time. The exam hall sometimes resembled a smokers' waiting room in a provincial railway station. There were no ashtrays, however, and I once set fire to one I improvised out of a page from the exam script, while musing on the finer points of a comparison between *Anna Karenina* and *Middlemarch*. I was aiming to impress my comparative literature professor by skiing off-piste. *Middlemarch* was definitely not on the syllabus. In Yugoslavia, George Eliot was mainly known for *The Mill on the Floss*, and was languishing in the twilight world of young adult fiction. Insinuating that she was equal to an obvious great such as Leo T. was a risky strategy, but I was a Dorothea still madly in love with Casaubon. I simply had to give it a go, I thought, as I drew in a mouthful of smoke. 'Colleague Bjelogrlic,' shouted the professor from the minstrels' gallery in the university's Hall of Heroes, which gave him a perfect view of a sea of students fidgeting over their papers, 'extinguish that fire at once, I say!'

Many of our professors addressed us with 'Colleague'. Others used 'Comrade', or 'Miss', according to whether they were communists or bourgeois recidivists. Forms of address provided an easy way of knowing individual political allegiances. It was useful to be able to distinguish Comrade Professors from Mr or Mrs Professors in order to know whether to cite Lukacs or T. S. Eliot. Although one could often tell the two groups apart simply by the clothes, it was not always safe to make hasty assumptions. Suits, ties and moccasins mostly belonged to comrades; tweed jackets, turtle necks and shoelaces to Mr and Mrs, but safari suits could go both ways, and were surprisingly popular in the early eighties.

———

The evening after the exam, Kosta made one of the strangest passes anyone has ever made at me. We were sitting in his father's library and drinking his father's wine when he took my left hand and started kissing the inside of my index finger, while repeating, 'Why not, why ever not?' in a strange, strangulated stage whisper. I wasn't sure whether he was trying to convince me, or was asking me to spell out the reasons why not, of which there were a million, but I thought his approach to courting quite original.

I stood up to leave and knocked against one of the heavy crystal lozenges of a large antique chandelier. I was some inches taller than Kosta (which might have been one of those million reasons why not). A rivulet of blood made its way from my forehead down my cheek and towards my lips. I ran into the lobby, still laughing and squealing with pain at the same time. Old Totitza, Kosta's family's ancient Slovak maid, rushed towards me, my coat at the ready in her hands, all the while repeating in a trembling, eighty-year-old voice, 'Are they OK, are they OK?' It took me a while to realize that she meant me, rather than her employers.

In pre-war Belgrade homes (pre-Second World War, that is), servants used to address their masters in the third-person plural. It didn't occur to me that my friend's father, a director of a big socialist cooperative and a member of the Communist Party since he was sixteen, encouraged such old-fashioned bourgeois etiquette in his house. When she finished wiping my brow with a linen tea towel, I gave Totitza a partisan salute. The scratch was barely visible. I was neither angry with Kosta nor particularly flattered. His countless amorous conquests depended on vast amounts of indiscriminate gunfire. His servant's anxious enquiries, however, were something to remind Kosta of now, particularly since she was long dead and he held the passport of a truly egalitarian state.

In the midst of laughter, Kosta suddenly looked at me quite seriously. My heart sank. I was by this stage so thoroughly attuned to English ways of flirting, which are quite different from the Serbian ones, that I briefly thought I might have encouraged some kind of declaration with which he was about to embarrass me. 'I keep trying to work out how you've changed. You sound the same, you've barely aged, you dress in a very similar way, and yet somehow you seem so much more English to me even when you speak Serbian. It must be the expression on your face,' he said. 'Back where we come from one doesn't smile so often, and one doesn't say everything is wonderful if it isn't.'

'Wonderful,' I retorted, and smiled.

My father's mother

What Kosta said worried me a bit. Much as I loved the English ways, I certainly did not want to cease being a Serb, whatever that implied. I was not reaching some Copernican, nationalist turning point. I simply felt that being English and Serbian at the same time was the only way I could now be happy: inside and outside, within and without, belonging but free. I wanted to remember every word in Serbian and keep learning the new ones. I needed to read and write in both languages, and to think in both, every day, in order not to forget the nuances of difference between the words which apparently meant the same thing.

That is how the idea of working for the BBC World Service initially came about. There were few Serbs in London who had both the radio experience and the necessary work permits to be in a position to accept the sequence of short-term work contracts of which the corporation, with its freshly discovered Thatcherism, was particularly fond. The BBC kept the option of getting rid of me at the drop of a hat, and I had the advantage of feeling like an insider without really belonging. I stayed with the World Service, on and off, for some seven years: longer, in fact, than I've ever spent working anywhere else. It says something about my spirit of contrariness that I was most willing to commit myself to those who kept dangling the get-out clause in front of my eyes.

203

The Serbian language service expanded in direct proportion to the spread of battlefields across the Balkans in the 1990s. The 'blink and you'll miss it' war in Slovenia in 1991 was followed by longer and far bloodier conflicts in Croatia and Bosnia, while the troubles of Kosovo and Macedonia bubbled quietly but insistently in the background, waiting for their own turn to explode. Detailed maps of my vanishing Yugoslav homeland appeared daily in British newspapers. The BBC needed Serbian voices like mine more than ever before. The belief which apparently stood behind the expansion in Serbian programming – that 'ordinary' people, misled by their nasty leaders, would mend their ways once given the right sort of information – seemed to me a touch too reliant on placing trust in the essential goodness of the human race, but what the hell. Someone had to keep tilting at the windmills, and I was as good as the next man.

Before I joined the BBC, I had a relatively vague notion of what its Yugoslav output was like. In so far as I had – while still resident in Belgrade – listened to its short-wave programmes on frequencies crackling with the static of the entire European mainland, it was in order to improve my English. Soon after I joined, the Serbo-Croat service split up, although the Serbs, the Croats, the Slovenes and the Macedonians remained loosely linked as a South Slavonic Service, a ghostly relic of the defunct state. Former Serbo-Croat broadcasters now went into either the Serbian or the Croatian room according to their accents. Thus a Serbian woman from Zagreb remained in the Croatian service, and a Macedonian speaking with a Belgrade accent continued his work in the Serbian section. There was no Bosnian programming and, as it happens, no Muslims were ever employed, so we divided our resident Bosnian Serbs and Croats between ourselves. No one complained. Under the caring eyes of our British bosses, we went forth and multiplied our programmes, as long as the wars went on. As soon as a country achieved peace and stability, the cutbacks began. No one could deny the justice in that: truth is not cheap, after all. If you can pay for it yourself, you should damn well be prepared to do so.

———

I went on with the job of translating news bulletins on the war in the Balkans and features on British life from English into Serbian, to the delight of my father-in-law, pleased that his son's wife was now effectively the voice of freedom and empire in the Balkans, and my mother, who remained one of my most faithful listeners in faraway Belgrade. As far as she was concerned, I was back on track to media fame. Radio was good, TV would have been even better.

A cohort of Serbian aunts, great-aunts and cousins remained glued to each of my radio appearances, and knew – from the minutest tremors in my voice – whether I was tired, unhappy or had a cold. They analysed each broadcast with all the skills of highly trained officials at Cheltenham's GCHQ, while paying little or no attention to the contents of my bulletins, which became increasingly depressing as the war progressed inexorably towards their own front doors. Even my little nephew taped one of my programmes and played it occasionally on his toy cassette recorder, shouting 'Auntie's on!' Before she wised up to his pranks, my mother tended to drop whatever else she was doing and run to the nearest radio. During my years at the Beeb, all the radios in our Belgrade home remained tuned to the World Service.

My familial audience was disappointed when I volunteered for an endless sequence of night shifts. I was hardly making the right career move by electing to read lullabies to Balkan insomniacs. Staying up all night wasn't good for my health, they pleaded, refusing to believe that I enjoyed the night duty, when I could be alone for some twelve hours. All the radio toys my sister and I had once dreamed of were now mine and mine alone: countless spools of brown, yellow and red-and-white tape, sharp razors to cut out unwanted speech from my recordings, computers humming with echoes of the troubled world outside, and cool, empty, sound-insulated studios behind whose padded doors I spoke and sang to myself to stay awake.

I wasn't avoiding my co-workers. They were a merry, largely lovable bunch of people who brought the best of my homeland right to the heart of London. Nonetheless, when no one told me what to do, I did the work much faster. I walked through the cavernous corridors of Bush House, past busy-looking people carrying bundles of tape-recordings, and along rows of dark rooms into which delivery men threw copies of morning newspapers with a muffled thud, setting off a sequence of automatically controlled lights.

From time to time, I went into the basement library to read poetry for a quarter of an hour. The rhymes echoed in my sleepy mind as it braced itself for the horrors of Balkan battlefields in the first dawn programmes. Every word and every image seemed strange. I read Auden's 'Night Mail' and thought not about the thousands asleep everywhere around me on this island, but about armoured columns preparing to move in on Bosnian villages while orders were being passed down the line, like invisible parcels of death, ready for delivery.

Between twelve thirty and three a.m., I took a nap in the dormitory, located in another of the basement warrens of Bush

House. The beds were separated from each other by curtains, like a hospital ward. You could always hear the night murmurs of broadcasters asleep. Simple grey blankets reminded me of army billets. At three o'clock precisely, a uniformed security guard came to wake me up by shining a small torch in my face, careful not to disturb the sleepers next to me. I hovered between wakefulness and sleep as I waited for my wake-up light, while sighs, snores and the soft rustle of bedding washed around me like waves.

At the same time, throughout the country which I still called my homeland innocent people huddled in the dark, afraid of the morning. At the BBC, I always seemed much closer to their pain than anywhere else in London, so close in fact that I felt it all the time. The radio waves which carried my voice channelled the suffering both outwards and inwards. I was my own most faithful listener, a hostage to the stories of death about which I could do nothing but transmit.

———

When I felt I could no longer fight sleep, I often stepped into the night streets of London. Freshly washed and empty, they belonged to me. So long as I looked as though I knew where I was going, no one ever bothered me. In fact – before I was temporarily confused by cancer – I always knew where I was going, so I never had any problems. I walked briskly around Bush House, which stood on night guard, flanked by the High Commissions of India and Australia like a forgotten soldier of the Commonwealth. Its white corporate flag, bearing the motto 'Nation shall speak peace unto nation', fluttered in the night wind, whipping the metal-tube mast, which echoed emptily.

On Kingsway, homeless people slept in cardboard boxes in office doorways, often in pairs, foot to foot or side by side. 'Hello, love,' called a male Irish voice from a flower-patterned sleeping bag on a neatly arranged mat of newspapers. 'Can't sleep. Can you?' 'I can't either,' I responded. In the quiet of the night, my voice sounded much more foreign for some reason. 'Where are you from?' the man continued. 'Russia,' I said, suddenly taken aback by the realization that I pretended to be Russian in order not to have to talk about the war in Yugoslavia. I obviously thought that, given half a chance, even a homeless person might ask, 'What the hell is going on down there?' 'Comrade Russki,' laughed the man instead, pulling his sleeping bag over his shoulders, 'Russia is finished, isn't it?' 'Finished? Maybe,' I replied and walked back towards the river, invisible but implicit behind the dark edifices and the sloping streets with their abrupt endings. I was right about his political bent after all.

I stared towards St Mary le Strand on its concrete island in the middle of a deserted street, like a plastic toy boat on the bottom of an empty bath. Traffic lights flickered at its flanks. Even at three a.m., the building of King's College, a block of unforgiving grey concrete, cast a gloomy shadow across the road. Its offices lined successive floors like human-sized pigeon-holes. I suddenly wanted to escape back to a place like that, simply to feel safe among books again. For some irrational reason, I thought that nothing bad could happen to me if I could just read and write, and talk about books. I wondered how many years it might take me to cross the road, but I sensed that the crossing had already begun. It was a strange move to be planning. Most people I knew seemed to want to come this way, towards the beckoning lights of the media, and expressed surprise when I mentioned my plans to teach. In Britain, teaching at any level – university included – is a relatively poorly paid job. In London, where lecturers' salaries barely cover the rent, it tends to be seen as a species of monasticism. For me, it represented a retreat to safety.

Much though I loved radio, the Yugoslav wars finally made me hate the news. I no longer wanted to know what was going on in the place from which I came. Ten years previously, I would buy a whole newspaper simply to read a five-line agency report from

Belgrade. Now that entire pages were devoted to it, I quickly turned over to Court & Social, Gardening, Motoring – anything. So long as the article did not contain the words Balkan, or war, or dead, it was fine.

Back in my office, a shoal of computer screens fringed with yellow Post-it notes shimmered in the dark like phosphorescent fish. From time to time, shadows of mice scuttled along the skirting boards, dodging traps, in search of biscuit crumbs. The office lights were set to switch off automatically when the sensors detected no movement. Bent over the keyboard, I regularly found myself engulfed in darkness. I kept forgetting to stand up and wave my arms about in order to turn the lights on and make the mice disappear.

No one visibly controlled my broadcasts, although everything I did was logged and recorded. 'Our victorious army entered the town yesterday,' said a colleague from the Croatian service, forgetting in his patriotic fervour that he was the voice of the BBC and not of some Zagreb outfit. Some days later, he had to explain himself to someone higher up the food chain. At Bush House we weren't really supposed to use 'our' for anything, British, Serbian, Croatian or anybody else's.

At the Serbian end of the enterprise I was less likely to make the same mistake. My Croatian colleague was only a few years younger than me, but the small difference in age had meant that he was educated in the dog days of Yugoslav socialism, when no one needed to pretend to worship the old gods of Titoism. Paradoxically, that seemed only to increase his desire to do obeisance to the new idols of nationalism. When we were growing up, my school friends and I had to write poems and essays about 'our army' – the one my father worked for – at what were practically monthly intervals: 20 October, Belgrade Liberation Day; 29 November, Republic Day; 22 December, Army Day. Our calendars were forever stuck in the early forties. We were never allowed to forget who – supposedly – liberated us from the occupying enemy and then held our Russian, American and British allies at bay. If the long years of commissioned rhymes achieved anything, they ensured that I never called any army mine in a hurry.

My news bulletins at the BBC were exemplary. Outwardly, I kept my distance and knew how to be even-handed. In my feelings about the war, however, I tended to overcompensate both in my distress that Serb suffering did not seem to register anywhere and in my shame that the Serbs could cause so much pain to others. Both suggested that my relationship with my own Serbianness was perhaps more raw than I admitted even to myself. It was part of a knotted circle of love and guilt which I preferred not to pick at very much. If I could have closed my eyes and kept Serbia beautiful, I would have done that, but before I knew it it was far too late.

———

In an echo of the world of Balkan politics, the BBC had given the Serbs and the Croats adjoining rooms, with no connecting doors but with a large window in the dividing wall, so that we could always see what the others were up to, although both sides feigned lack of interest as they went about their daily work. The Croatian section overlooked the street; the Serbian faced a large pillar through pigeon mesh. The Serbs therefore needed more light, which they could only get if they had a window in the Croatian wall. Was the management trying to send some kind of message?

One night in early August 1995, one of my colleagues from the Croatian service, who bore a very grand Montenegrin name, came into the Serbian office to tell me to hold the top news story for the morning bulletin. His sources reported that something big was about to happen in the Serb-held enclave of Knin. By five a.m., that 'something' became operation 'Storm'; columns of the Croatian army advanced towards Knin, while inside it thousands of Serbs prepared to flee. After I read the news, I locked myself in a cubicle in the women's lavatory. Tears ran down my face, leaving big wet blotches on my white shirt. I cried for the bewildered refugees in their endless columns moving east, and then I cried that I didn't cry in the same way when others suffered. I realized that I could still tell 'my side' simply by how much it hurt.

I had the answer to Kosta's question. I had become English in every possible way, but the fault lines along which the pain reached me were still Serbian, whatever that may imply. This is not to say that I forgave my fellow Serbs for any of the awful things they had done in the Balkan wars, or that I forgave myself for anything I could have done to help but didn't, simply that the me I had created, that fashionable, travelling, global, postmodern subject of my own little life story, had a chink in her armour after all. The truth, the real story, and all the other journalistic fictions and pretensions seemed irrelevant by comparison.

I joined the BBC in order to keep my mother tongue alive, and I now knew more words for dying than the Inuit know for snow. I had to admit, although that wasn't news, that I wasn't really made to be a news hound. I took things to heart. I kept looking at them from both sides, until nothing seemed clear any more. By owning up to my own weakness, I conceded the feeling of moral superiority to anyone who felt able to throw any certainty at me. I had none, except perhaps for the knowledge that, if an army was created, it would go to war sooner or later. I was about to disappoint my mother again. I kept escaping to the British Library to work on a book about the Balkan past with much more enthusiasm than I ever had for the Balkan present. Whatever I now needed to learn must certainly be there.

Belgrade, winter 1984

Some months before my nineteenth birthday, I was invited to read a poem on Studio B, then Belgrade's most fashionable radio station. I was no stranger to poetry readings but I was not prepared for the magic of radio. When she heard the music fade under her voice, the shy exhibitionist in me – a creature of contradictions – knew she had found a home, a place to be invisible and show off at the same time. I stayed on to present a programme aimed at secondary school students, called *An Extra Hour*, through my last school year and the summer before going to university. Studio B could barely be heard beyond the boundary marked by the orbital road around Belgrade, but this was still my entire world anyway.

My fellow presenter, a nursing student called Ljuba, was a tall, lanky youth whose voice was as clear as crystal. He and I read the news from Belgrade schools, interviewed young athletes and maths champions, and, in between, played modish tunes. I was part of the most stylish crowd in the world, I was regularly being asked out by some of the most fantastic-looking young men around, and I was just eighteen. Even my parents extended the curfew from eleven to eleven thirty when I argued that I needed the extra half-hour in order to review the latest theatrical openings and still get home by public transport: what more could a girl ask for? I didn't know where the top of the world was, but it couldn't have been far away.

For our editor, once a star radio presenter, this might have been a career cul-de-sac. For Ljuba and me, it was heaven on earth, a world straight out of the communist Utopia, in which you worked purely because you loved work – 'from each according to his abilities, to each according to his needs' – except that we were not paid a penny. *The Extra Hour* was in many ways a typical creation of the socialist media. Its main purpose was to train new generations of radio presenters. I never knew whether I had an audience of two or two million: there was no pressure of that kind. The programme existed simply because someone once thought it was a good idea. I was truly a spoilt child of communism in so far as I was brought up never to worry about where the money was coming from. It was simply there when you needed it. Then it ran out.

My mother and father hoped that my career on Studio D might lead to all sorts of things, although finally it led to nothing very much, other than a brief moment of radio fame inside the Belgrade orbital. In fact, my parents have always had an over-riding concern with exactly where things might lead. Their very different family backgrounds were similar in their poverty, and in the restrictions socialism placed on their early freedom of choice. In their view, any action I took was inseparable from its potential, distant consequences. Any boy with whom I went out to dance was analysed as a prospective husband, any two-day job as a career for life. My momentary whims and my thirst for new experiences – the way I abandoned men and places and projects, expecting that the next one would be waiting for me just around the corner; the way I said I needed to 'try everything'; even the way I spoke my mind – were alien to their instinct to hold on to what you already had. 'Don't run from the first one,' my mother kept saying, and yet I always did, particularly when there was no good reason for it.

While youthful experiences of hunger and dispossession made my parents long for stability and permanence, the days of my own early life clicked and clacked into each other steadily and predictably, like rows of worry beads. You could always see the next bead on the string, bright and shiny and almost identical to the one you'd just held with your fingertips. Once I tasted war, illness and unhappiness, I too changed my prayers from *give* to *please don't take away*. There were things, all too many things, I found out, which I wouldn't really want to try, not even once.

'Now that my daughter-in-law is a journalist,' my father-in-law says, 'Would she mind taking a look at my *Piffer* column?' We are talking colleague-to-colleague here – the producer of the BBC Serbian Service to a correspondent of *The Piffer*, the newsletter of the Punjab Frontier Force, to which my father-in-law contributed a regular diary piece. It is more than half a century since he left India as part of the withdrawal of the British legions. He was still in his early twenties. After partition, in which *his* corner of India became Pakistan, there were years at Cambridge, years of active service in Malaya and Singapore, years of running a farm in Surrey and years of retirement in an ancient house in Sussex, surrounded by apple orchards, but those years somehow counted for less. The British may have left the Asian subcontinent, but my father-in-law's heart and mind were still in the rocky borderlands with Afghanistan where he served amid the ebb tide of the Raj.

As a foreigner from a poor country which was itself a kind of colony throughout most of its history, I cannot grasp the attraction of, and even less the homesickness for, India of the kind which I first encountered when I met my father-in-law. Several generations of men in my husband's family abandoned beautiful houses amid the southern English hills, which roll towards the coast like opalescent waves, for life in khaki tents on sun-blasted plateaux in Asia and Africa. Granted, there were grand army titles, and governorships of strange places, and lots and lots of medals, or in a word – one of my father-in-law's favourite Urdu words – *izzat* (honour), but that life seems to have brought them little money and less love, and these were the only reasons, as far as I was concerned, why anyone would desire to live abroad.

Simon's great-grandfather

I had been a communist and a Tory and ended up as a typecast university lecturer: mistrustful of political parties and a leftist liberal. I vote Green to put pressure on whoever is in government, but if the Greens ever came anywhere near real power I would probably want to vote for someone else. Regardless of changes in perspective, my father-in-law's India story has never entirely made sense to me. This is perhaps because I have, in some way which is still beyond my grasp, remained an alien, even if I now understand how a love of England, her milky greenness fed by months of melancholy rain, can thrive at a distance of several thousand miles.

I scan the vast library behind my father-in-law's desk: copies of New Calcutta directories, of army lists and of what seems like just about every book on India ever published. The walls are adorned with prints of expeditions to places I didn't know existed and of wars of which I've never even heard – the battle of Goojerat, the storming of Mooltan, the battle of Sobraon. The room is a link to an earlier Britain whose pulse barely beats; but the country of which I am now part still loves its soldiers and parades, its shiny buttons and its metal toys, more than any other place in Europe, except perhaps for Serbia and Russia.

I edit his article, a list of updates from old India hands and officers' widows: illnesses, moves to old people's homes in places like Cheltenham and Chichester, and deaths, several deaths in every column. Amid all this I realize that my husband's father is now, in many ways, as much an exile in Britain as I am. We understand each other so well not because I am a journalist and journalists adore soldiers, and not because we are bound by the same name and the love of his son, but because we both belong here and somewhere else, to places and times and countries which no longer exist. We are linked by a homesickness which doesn't make sense.

———

To break a long sequence of night bulletins and Balkan battles, I decide to visit the North-West Frontier Province with my husband and his father. We stay with my father-in-law's friends, retired officers of the Pakistani Army, in an Islamic version of the world of Tolstoy's novels. Martial, equestrian, latifundia-owning Pathans, they speak English and travel the world. The gulf between them and their villagers is just as great as between Bezukhov and his serfs. Among orange and mango orchards on distant country estates, I discover houses with libraries which echo my father-in-law's collection. They provide lavish shelters from the bleak villages and herds of emaciated cattle, so far removed from the dusty roads on which boys in rags play cricket after a long day's work that they might as well be in Dorset.

My father-in-law is happy, as happy as I've ever seen him be. His Urdu is rusty, his Pushto is a joke, but he is at home. In England, he often descends into long silences, but in the large households of Peshawar, Islamabad and Rawalpindi he seems never to run out of conversation. He wants to know all about government manoeuvrings, internecine Islamic clashes, reforms and road building plans, and hundreds of other details. Britain simply does not interest him any longer in this way.

He takes me to visit a hospital, a cotton factory and even a gun workshop in Tribal Territory, where the government's writ does not run and a faithful replica of any weapon you bring can be made overnight for a few rupees. My head is covered but my mouth is not: he smiles proudly when I boast of my own prowess as a markswoman, even though I am not sure quite what I'm trying to prove.

I often have to watch him and my husband from an unaccustomed distance, seated among women in ornate *shalwar kamiz* and expensive gold jewellery. One of them quizzes me, amiably but relentlessly, about the reasons why I don't have children. She shakes her head when I say I don't know. When we bid our

farewells, she whispers, 'May God give you a son next year,' into
my ear.

I marvel at the beautiful century which could bring a Serbian
girl, a former commie, to the verandas lining the northern edges
of the Asian subcontinent in the company of an old Englishman
who fought communists in the jungles of Malaya. In the long
evenings, over dried mulberries and cups of sweet tea, I start to
show him books I brought with me on the journey, writings by
Sara Suleri, Pankaj Mishra, Anita Desai – the sort of India I
know about – but he is tired after a day's walking and dozes off
in the middle of my story. My husband chuckles quietly in the
corner, his face hidden behind a thick history book.

I ask the servant to prepare my bed, then walk over to the
room to give a helping hand. I succeed only in embarrassing the
poor man. It's too late to learn how to be gracefully feudal. When
I return outside, the sky is lit with hundreds of stars and for a
moment the last call to prayer overpowers the crackling chimes
of Big Ben on the BBC World Service, to which my father-in-law,
awake again, listens in semi-darkness on my husband's small
transistor radio. The news bulletin is presented by someone I
know well. On the other side of the world, where the day is still

unspent, I see the basement studio of Bush House, and a freckled, serious face behind the microphone. From this distance, I feel that I too am listening to the voice of home. 'I'll forgive you your wars, if you forgive mine' is something I don't say to my father-in-law. There is no need.

My father-in-law (tallest, as ever) with two of his brothers at Eton

8

FATHERS AND SONS

The day of my father-in-law's funeral was one of those sunny, translucent English summer days when everything stands still for a moment. The air was full of pollen, petals and fragrance, as though someone had turned the earth – with London on it – upside down and back again, like a snowstorm in a paperweight. Even the slopes of Kensal Green cemetery, in an otherwise bleak corner of north-west London, looked so fecund and lush that it seemed as if the Victorian stone angels had gathered for a picnic on broken gravestones scattered like sugar cubes among wild flowers and tall grasses.

I watch the small groups of white-haired men and women gather around my husband and his brother in front of the cemetery chapel. The mourners are so unmistakably English that they might have been painted by Gainsborough two centuries earlier. Fresh from their trains at Victoria and Charing Cross, they look alien and out of place, as though London is a foreign town, to be negotiated with care. Many of the men wear silk neckties with colourful regimental stripes and highly polished, thick-soled shoes which fall on the ground with a heavy parade sound. Even in retirement, they look as though they are in uniform. 'Indian Army,' whispers one experienced chapel attendant to another.

My father-in-law's long, long coffin is carried into the chapel. No one displays visible signs of grief, although it is somehow clear that the occasion is a mournful one. At a Belgrade family funeral, someone would have been wailing at this point. Other mourners would have audibly stifled their sobs in the pauses between orations, or sighed heavily against the low monotone of the Orthodox chant. Here, we open our hymn books and sing at the prompt given by the organist.

I am not familiar with the tunes and pay too much attention to the Victorian verse, which is at the same time touchingly beautiful and too upbeat about death for my taste. The celebration of departure, the refusal to accept separation as anything but a brief interlude, makes it sound as though my father-in-law is off to plant a Union flag in the sands of some paradise island. I stumble over the lines, catching up and losing the melody. I can't get myself to sing at an Anglican funeral, just as I couldn't – were it an Orthodox one – wail as my female ancestors were expected to. In Serbia old women were sometimes even paid to mourn. They walked behind the coffin in the funeral procession and celebrated the dead in wailing laments delivered in rhythmic, haunting pentameters. I am stuck somewhere between the singing and the wailing, speechless.

My father-in-law during his farming days

I am, although no one but me knows it yet, exactly one week pregnant. My father-in-law collapsed suddenly, of internal bleeding, on the night of 28 June 1999. That evening, in a sudden flash of intuition, I had announced to my husband that I wasn't going to see in my thirty-eighth birthday childless. After thirteen years of marriage – and with only two days to go before the birthday in question – my husband knew better than to contradict, although he has always had little time for intuition of this kind. This is one of those moments in which the difference between the two worlds we come from shows most clearly. In his, destiny is something you are supposed to take into your own hands. In mine, it falls like a block of concrete from the open sky.

Is it surprising that we then try to second guess moments of triumph and disaster by staring into the dregs of coffee at the bottom of a cup we have drunk, or at haphazardly thrown handfuls of beans, or the shoulder blades of slaughtered animals? We deal in revelations and epiphanies in order to mask powerlessness: intimations of the future do not fully translate between my Eastern and my Western world. I am never sure whether to believe them either, but visions are the stock in trade of my Montenegrin family. One of the clans I hail from – the Prorokovic, literally the sons of prophets – throws up seers in every generation. I suspect by now that I am not one of the elect, but I often get it right nonetheless.

I wake up in the middle of the night feeling an unfamiliar electric buzz in the pit of my stomach. 'This is it,' I say to myself. 'A child.' Then the phones begin to ring, bringing the news of my father-in-law's death. In the days which follow, amid the rush of funeral arrangements, I forget about the strange, glorious moment of my son's conception, but I feel different all the time. In the cemetery chapel I know for certain that I am no longer one but two. No bigger than a tadpole by the time I turn thirty-eight, the child waits for the century to come to an end.

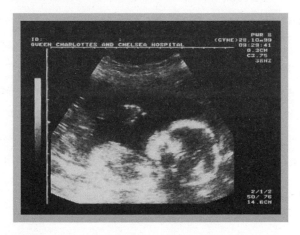

My son, Alexander, waiting to be born

After the funeral service, we walk towards the cluster of Goldsworthy graves under the crowns of mature chestnut trees. One or two monuments cover empty lots, preserving the memory of men and women whose bodies lie in places like Calcutta and the Indian Ocean. The lettering has faded and we have to guess what the Victorian palimpsest adds up to. The most recent grave, built on the eve of the First World War, contains three generations of fathers, sons and their wives. For some reason, the family I married into seems always to have had four or five boys to each girl. Even in the cemetery, the world I am inscribing myself into seems overwhelmingly masculine and spartan to the core. I sit on the edge of a salmon-coloured marble square and read the rows of old-fashioned names around me: Walter, Roger, Everard, Frederick, Charlotte, Sophia, Mary Emma. I try to insert Vesna into the sequence. In 1999, this still seems an amusing thought. An eternity, uninterrupted, stretches ahead of me.

In the adjacent plot, three gleaming new black gravestones occupy what must once have been a cemetery path. Their gold Cyrillic lettering tells of Serbs exiled in London after the Second World War. One proclaims loyalty to the deposed king; one pays a tribute to Mum and Dad; the third simply marks the beginning and the end, a village in Bosnia and a suburb on the road to

231

Heathrow Airport. I take a black scarf out of my pocket, cover my hair and say a short Orthodox prayer for the dead. Finally, the tears arrive.

———

For some years now, I have bidden farewell to my parents at the boarding gates of different airports, thinking, in no longer than the briefest of moments, that this hug, this kiss, this goodbye, might well be the last. I observe my father slowing down, or suddenly notice that my mother's eyes are the eyes of an old woman, and wonder, guiltily, whether he or she will be the first to go. Although they live in a land where people grow older sooner, and die younger, so long as they are together I remain a child, and I am not sure I know how to be anything else. It is a measure of my sheltered, protected life that it never even occurs to me that the order of departure might be any different from the order of arrival.

When I am told I have cancer, it takes three days before I can make the telephone call to let Mother and Father know. I wonder whether they really need to be told. I don't know what to expect. They belong to the generation which hid this illness like a guilty secret, through mortal fear, taboo and superstition. I find out that cousins and neighbours had died from it only once

I join the club myself, but I also get to hear stories of miraculous survival. I hug a ninety-year-old woman, an old family friend, feeling, for the first time, a breast that is not there. 'And it hasn't been for over forty years,' she suddenly confides, timid but unyieldingly triumphant, like a girl.

When I finally do tell them, I cannot quite work out whether my parents are fantastically brave or in denial about what I'm going through. Their telephone calls are upbeat and full of a kind of Blitz spirit which opens no cracks for the possibility of defeat. 'How are you today, my son?' my mother asks cheerfully after each dose of chemotherapy I receive. In Serbian, calling a daughter 'my son', 'my brave son' – using the masculine as a generic name for a child – is not that unusual. With my bald, smooth head and my fresh operation scars, I look more like a son than ever before. If only she could see me. Apropos of nothing much, my shy, reticent father tells me that having me for a daughter is the best thing that has ever happened to him.

Gradually I begin to understand something about courage and denial. I decide to join the Blitz brigade myself. I won't hide my wounds – I am too proud for that – but I shall be the brightest glow-worm in the radiotherapy department. I shall fight it wherever. I shall never surrender. You sing or wail if you like, I'll just keep mum.

My twenties and my thirties were spent in a state of extended adolescence. The motto of those two decades could have been 'There's still plenty of time'. I held a sequence of fine, untroubling jobs. I never felt I was working hard, perhaps because, unlike my parents and even more unlike my grandparents, I had the luxury of never having to do anything I didn't like for very long. Looking back from where I am now, everything seems fantastically, unbearably easy.

Perhaps because of that ease, I deliberately sought difficulty. I travelled the world in a way which often confused my mother and father. Staying in fine hotels in places like Vienna or Paris was one thing, but seeking austere lodgings in the shadows of the Atlas, Ararat or K-2, as I began to do, was more difficult to understand. The luxury of deliberate hardship was not something my parents could begin to grasp. There lies a real generation gap. They could not understand my need to take risks simply in order to have a story to tell. This is the measure of my Western hubris, perhaps.

In the first days of 1990, Simon and I interrupted a Christmas visit to Belgrade in order to witness the revolution in Romania while the body of Ceausescu, Romania's freshly executed communist dictator, was still warm. Father drove us to the Danube Station to catch an empty train east. Our old Skoda coughed through the snowdrifts like a tubercular patient, and, in the back, Mother begged me not to stray too far from the hotel. In a freezing Bucharest room, lit by the moonlight refracted in the icicles hanging from the roof of the hotel, we listened to the echoing sounds of street demonstrations and ate sandwiches that Mother had furtively squeezed into our rucksacks before departure.

I was grateful for her foresight: there was barely any food in the Romanian capital, and even that which was available was inedible. The soft white buns with delicate slices of salami, cheese and sweet roast pepper, carefully layered to create a chequerboard effect, were both extravagant and so perfectly telling of the ways in which Mother inscribed her love into our lives. It both infuriated and moved beyond words. After all, this was the woman who, before she went to work at five ten in the morning, found the energy to create elaborate swirls in mayonnaise on the ham and cheese *tartines* she left on the table ready for her daughters' breakfast two hours later, simply because she thought that the swirls might encourage my sister to eat.

We returned from Bucharest with photographs of rows of wax candles still burning on the sites of recent sniper killings, of tanks encircling the TV station, flags with the communist star cut out, smouldering ruins. The people in the streets of Bucharest celebrated the end of tyranny, intoxicatingly free for a moment. Back in Belgrade, the death spasms of communism, which thousands celebrated with unmitigated joy, made my parents worry about what would follow. Change was something to be feared. They had lived their entire lives in a world in which every regime seemed bound to be worse than the previous one. In Serbia, that seemed to sum up the entire twentieth century.

———

For years, my mother and my aunts kept asking me about the children who weren't arriving. Why would one marry, if not to have a child? From their point of view, I was already alarmingly old for first-time motherhood at twenty-seven, let alone ten years later. In the meantime, at two- or three-yearly intervals, Simon and I had a conversation about parenthood which usually ended with, 'There's still plenty of time.' I wanted to complete my doctorate, I wanted to write a book, I wanted to see what would happen. I wanted all manner of things, some more selfish than others. I wanted a child too, but there was still plenty of time for that.

My first birthday

The Yugoslav war went on for almost eight years. Even when we tried not to mention it, it was there like a body buried in our back garden. We talked about *that*, *out there*, we tried to guess what was *really* happening, we argued over who or what was to blame: insiders, outsiders, those who stayed behind, those who – like me – left the country, religious fanatics or godless communists, us or them. Yugoslavia was simultaneously the only solution and the worst of all possible worlds. I couldn't decide whether I loved or hated it. I had hauntingly beautiful memories of that country, yet it appears that it was also, and for so many people, an ugly, doomed place.

I often returned home from work just in time to watch the landscapes of my childhood burn on the early-evening television news. Every now and then I saw familiar faces. A high-school friend flitted briefly across the screen in a flak jacket, running across a square in Prishtina. I had no idea what he was doing there. A theatre director pointed to the burning edifice of Sarajevo Town Hall and I recognized the bandy-legged boy who took me out skating years ago. The spokeswoman for the Bosnian Ministry of Defence was, I realized, the young Muslim journalist whom I met in a restaurant on the Adriatic coast one sweltering August evening. We exchanged confidences over steaming bowls of mussels and glasses of cold beer, as one does only with complete strangers. Our great secrets – the reasons for the early breakdown of her marriage in a small town in eastern Bosnia, the intricacies of the complicated love-life I delighted in when I was twenty-two – seem now to belong to someone else, yet I can still recall them word for word. I felt that she was a kindred spirit, a sister-soul.

238

———

'Don't you remember Radovan?' my father asks one day. My Montenegrin clan is connected by marriage to the Karadzic clan, and Radovan, the leader of the Bosnian Serbs, used to turn up at family weddings and funerals before he became wanted by the armies of the world for a list of war crimes as long as my arm. I don't really remember Radovan, but he reminds me how painfully I remain tied to the war even at over a thousand miles' distance, through webs of family and friendship which seem to stretch as far back as I can remember.

I want to get closer to the conflict in order to understand it, then I think that my distance and my confusion are the only possible means of understanding. I have brief Martha Gellhorn moments when I go off to the Balkans in search of truth. I pay to be driven around by unshaven thugs who peruse the glossy product catalogue of Heckler & Koch while I walk forlornly on the edges of bomb craters hoping to see God knows what. I have Virginia Woolf moments when I escape to Sussex to collect large polished pebbles on the beach, just in case. Then I look up to the sky and wonder why I wasn't born in Denmark. 'Bad luck, girl,' comes the reply out of nowhere. 'Deal with it.' This is as close as I ever get to any kind of epiphany. And I do. I deal with it.

Then it – the body in the garden – starts moving closer. One evening, returning home from the theatre, I meet a neighbour's sixteen-year-old boy in the street and he says, 'Did you hear the news? We've started bombing Serbia tonight.' His father is Serbian and his mother English: that *we* obscures a thousand contradictions. I rush into the house and dial my mother and father's number with a desperate sense of urgency although there is nothing to say, just as I would – for as long as NATO bombers flew over Belgrade – continue to ring them every day simply to say hello. It is the only thing I can do. It is a ritual like not stepping on the cracks in paving stones, pure superstition, a compulsion. If I don't get through, they will die.

A week into the bombing, my sister wonders whether to take her family away from Belgrade and back to Toronto, where she had lived in the early nineties. 'Go. Just go. As far west and as far north as you can bear to go,' I urge her. Even in London I feel too close. She leaves the bombed city, and there are agonizing hours while she and her children travel by bus – along exposed highways and across bridges which might or might not be of interest to NATO's pilots – north to Hungary. Although the skies above Serbia are the busiest in Europe, the kind of plane she needs no longer flies there. She calls to say that they've made it across the border – no one hit, no one taken off the bus – and then they fly over me in London and across the Atlantic. For the rest of the spring, I call both Belgrade and Toronto, at different ends of the day.

———

In those daily calls during the bombing season, it is my father who keeps the laughter alive. With my sister and her children gone, Mother is like a flame extinguished, yet Father suddenly makes the war seem nothing if not funny. He has seen it all before, he claims. His Second World War stories have a Mark Twain-like glow of childhood memory, and a whatever-happens-now-I've-seen-worse stoicism. We laugh for long minutes before one of us puts the receiver down. 'Whatever could you have found so funny?' ask my husband and my mother in unison, at different ends of the transcontinental line. The fact that the telephone connections between my two warring countries remain open is a little miracle in itself.

Father had already seen two aerial attacks on Belgrade on Easter Day: the Germans bombed in 1941, when he was eight, and the Allies in 1944. They went for many of the places NATO is targeting today. 'Third time lucky,' Father says when the oil refinery in the river valley explodes, emitting a large, black, mushroom cloud. 'Your mother will have to wash the curtains now.' On British television, where I watch them, the direct hits sound strangely muted, like the crack of a bicyclist's skull hitting the asphalt. 'I may be an orphan at sixty-six but at least I no longer have my mother to worry about, only yours,' Father says.

I once thought of Father's generation of men as cowards simply because they allowed the communists to rule unchallenged for so many years. I admired the Czechs and the Hungarians, who climbed on to the Soviet tanks in those grainy black-and-white documentaries, and thought of them as much more courageous than the Serbs, the Croats and the rest of the Yugoslav lot. Now I wonder if I was right. I realize how much easier it is to climb on an enemy tank than to know exactly what to do with your own. My generation of spoilt, well-travelled, English-speaking socialist kids has hardly done much better.

'Christ is risen, Daddy,' I shout from west London on a Sunday morning. 'He is risen indeed,' Father shouts back from Serbia, against the wailing sound of air-raid sirens. There is no reason to interrupt the conversation. My parents stay away from air-raid shelters. The phone lines crackle but remain alive and I continue to call once a day, to ward off the evil eye. Then the war stops. The British Army advances into Prishtina, and it is an ending of sorts. 'It's somebody else's worry now,' I tell my parents, but this is true only up to a point. I don't want to see British soldiers dying. I am British too.

———

My father was the only man in a household of strong women. He negotiated between two headstrong daughters, his wife and his mother with the skills of an experienced peace negotiator. Like the UN, he risked unpopularity all the time. Whenever there was a prohibition to be prescribed, my mother urged us to 'ask your father', unwilling ever to say no herself. If she wanted to get her mother-in-law to comply with anything, she always sent Father to do the explaining: why, for example, it was unwise for Granny to take three times the recommended dose of Mother's blood pressure-lowering pills when her blood pressure was already extremely low (Granny loved taking tablets just as much as she hated going to the doctor and would swallow a handful of whatever happened to be around); or why it wasn't necessary to knit woollen stockings for the entire family and even less to undo perfectly nice jumpers in order to get the wool for the stockings. Granny didn't take kindly to lessons of this kind. She saw them as direct personal attacks, to which she responded with equally direct denunciations of Father, in which she

243

referred to things that only a mother would know about her son. My father, an angel of patience where she was concerned, tended to react with a long, imperturbable, 'Mama, please.'

Most of the time, however, Granny watched over Father's interests with the eyes of a hawk. The hierarchy of her affections was always abundantly clear. We were her family, but he was her body and soul. He was her only child, after all. Even when Father was in his fifties and Granny in her seventies, she urged us to ensure that we never let him leave the house without a scarf or a pair of gloves, as if she was trying to make up for his childhood years, when she dug the fields all day and sewed shirts for money all night, bent over the neck of her Singer machine in the rising waves of white cotton like a rider in a desperate race against the tide. 'You're abandoning Misha,' she said sadly while she watched me pack for England, as though I was leaving a child behind.

———

Halfway through the Second World War, in the middle of Zharkovo marketplace, where she was selling her agricultural produce, Granny hit a junior German officer on the head with a heavy key. Her German was poor but evidently good enough for an argument. She was promptly locked away, for all anyone knew to await execution. For hours, my good grandfather pleaded with the local mayor to intercede, and the mayor in turn pleaded with the German authorities. They finally let her go, quite possibly believing that she had to be mad because she refused to apologize. Her response to her release was pure, unmitigated anger. Her husband – my grandfather – should not have pleaded with anyone as far as she was concerned; and it was typical of his weakling nature that he had even contemplated such a thing.

Grandfather is often curiously absent from my family story. Born in the last decade of the nineteenth century, he seems to belong to a different historical era from the rest of us. He appears, in walk-in parts, in stories in which he usually tries to appease Granny's fiery temper. 'A fool,' Granny repeats lovingly, decades after his death.

On 19 October 1944, a gang of Soviet soldiers barely out of their teens burst into Granny's kitchen in the southern suburbs of Belgrade, demanding to be fed. She went out into the backyard, caught a hapless chicken, beheaded it with an axe and plunged it, still half-covered in feathers, into a pot of boiling water. Minutes later, the Soviet boys devoured the bird, barely warmed through, expressed appreciation and moved on towards the city, which echoed with exploding shells. In Granny's book the Soviets were the good guys, part of the Orthodox International. When my then eleven-year-old father sat down to his usual wartime meal of watery polenta, Granny slapped a spoonful of plum jam on his plate, to 'celebrate the end of the Schwab'. (For her generation, all Germans and all Austrians were Swabian.) The following day, Belgrade was taken by the communists. Or freed. It depends on your point of view.

When I ask my father what he remembers of the Second World War, he tells me how he became a film buff by attending dozens of free screenings of Nazi movies in the local cinema. This is a deliberately sunny, father-like memory of war. 'They were great films,' my father says. His passion for cinema, initiated though it may have been by Goebbels's propaganda, remains one of his most endearing traits. When I was a child, we saw literally hundreds of films together. He took me to the children's shows at the Yugoslav Army Club every Sunday morning, and we often saw one or two films in the city during the week: it was, supposedly, the best way to keep my sister and me away from under Mother's busy feet.

In summer, we went to the garden cinema of the Officers' Club in the Unknown Hero Street, just across the road from us, almost every evening. This was the most beautiful cinema in the world: heady with the smell of jasmine and tobacco and lit by thousands of stars. The performances were punctuated at ten-minute intervals by the sound of trolleybuses coming to a halt in the street just outside the wire fence hidden by lilac bushes. The first few rows of garden chairs were always filled with children. Every evening we went to bed with a deep imprint of woven plastic on the backs of our thighs. No one paid much attention to the guidance ratings: we saw whatever film happened to be on.

When our parents were too tired to take us to the cinema, we joined the ranks of neighbourhood kids for a free viewing through the wire at the other side of the screen. Struggling to read the subtitles backwards boosted our language skills. The crunching of the gravel under the rows of chairs where the adults sat on the other side of the white canvas usually announced an imminent love scene. We giggled our way through long embraces until a parent came to shoo us off. There was never any nudity in the films we saw – at least not until some time in the mid-seventies – but the passion was there, all the time.

My parents in their mid-twenties

In their choice of films, my parents remained true to their gender stereotypes. Mother loved old-style romantic weepies, while Father preferred *films policiers*, Westerns and war epics, Yugoslav, Russian and American alike. With him, we chased the Redskins across the prairies one evening and raced to plant the hammer-and-sickle banner on the Reichstag the next. With her, it was always the long farewells, the promises of undying love, the deathbed scenes. When they took us to see a film together, they tended to compromise by choosing Italian comedies and French costume dramas. Joint cinema outings were more sophisticated by default. In fact, the movies connected my parents' generation to ours with a shared pool of celluloid references.

248

None of my four grandparents had ever set foot in the cinema.

Father often quoted his favourite hard-boiled detectives, and my sister and I answered back faster than the wisecracking fifties dames. Mother could never decide which film star to compare her beautiful daughters to. While my slim sister was likened to the sweet child stars like Shirley Temple or *gamine* actresses like Audrey Hepburn, the plumper me seemed destined for similes with old-time divas and sultry neo-realist Italian beauties. 'Isn't she just like Ava Gardner in *The Snows of Kilimanjaro*?' Mother asked an aunt of mine when I was barely twelve. 'I'd say *Mogambo*,' suggested the aunt for reasons known only to her. 'How about Ita Rina?' my sister threw the name of one of Serbia's silent-movie stars into the game. They paused for a moment. No one was certain about Ita Rina's precise looks, but everyone knew the name, which has featured in every crossword puzzle as 'famous Serbian actress (7)' for as long as anyone can remember.

With his dark eyes, his glossy black hair and his trim moustache, Father had the good looks of an earlier, black-and-white era. Our neighbours – his erstwhile school friends – often told us that he was quite a heart-breaker in those mythical days before we were born. I was never quite sure what that meant. In the early seventies, when he was barely forty, Father's hair went white almost overnight and he shaved off the moustache. He suddenly looked incredibly Slav, like a young member of the Politburo or a colonel in the Red Army.

———

We took most of our holidays in Yugoslavia, in the Yugoslav National Army's own resorts and hotels in the mountains or by the sea. Closing the house for a trip to the Adriatic was one of our summer rituals. Unlike Mother, who always dreamed of journeys to an odd assortment of places which mapped out her own adolescent dreams (Paris, Geneva, Madeira, Nice), Father only ever left home with a heavy heart. He travelled abroad most reluctantly. Occasional trips to Italy and Greece were hard-won concessions to his daughters.

Father not only had to ask for permission from his employer before going abroad but had to write detailed reports on his movements and contacts. The army was understandably a bit worried that its code-breakers might break an unexpected code or two. His patient trails with his daughters through Roman department stores probably made a less than riveting read for some weary officer back home.

In fact, Father hardly ever spoke to anyone, while my sister and I chattered eagerly in English, French and Italian, and Mother smiled benevolently towards us. He was perhaps different only on a long train journey across the Soviet Union which we undertook one summer, where everyone addressed him in Russian without a second thought, and he responded in a fluent, almost accentless stream. He had a special talent for conversations in which he revealed nothing in the most charming way possible. 'When will Yugoslavia finally send a man into space?' asked a drunken Russian train conductor one night. 'Will it be with us or the Americans?' 'The more important question just now is which planet to go for,' Father replied.

———

'What will happen when I marry Simon?' I asked Father in the autumn of 1984. 'Could you lose your job?'

I was genuinely worried. I had been free to come and go as I pleased, more or less my entire life, and I'd made friends in both the East and the West, but I knew so little of the world he disappeared into every day.

'You do what you have to do,' Father answered. I was not sure that he really knew how his bosses would respond, but he kept his job. He was due to retire in two or three years' time, but by then it wouldn't have mattered anyway. The Yugoslav army had greater things to worry about than an English son-in-law.

———

Then the new century begins and Alexander is born. On a sunny day in early March 2000, Simon takes him from hospital in a big, bright blue-and-orange pram. I am driven home, less than a mile away, all milk and blood. On a west London street, I look out of the car towards the brand-new father and his brand-new boy under the rainbow-coloured parasol. Nothing can go wrong now. Nothing.

9

ENGLAND, MY ENGLAND

Early one morning, I am wheeled into the operating theatre with a green paper bracelet bearing my name, date of birth and gender (a succinct biography) on each of my wrists. 'In case they become separated,' I tell the anaesthetist. His smile is the last thing I see for some ten hours. When I open my eyes again, it's already evening. I am all there: one aching, motionless piece of flesh. This is my second major operation in less than a year. I am familiar with the ways in which the body which has been cut, opened and sewn up begins to heal itself. Hours translate into a handful of days, each one as long as eternity. Time stretches and compresses itself in patterns drawn by pain.

In my morphine-fuelled hospital dreams it rains all night, steadily, incessantly, just as it is supposed to rain in England. My body is a map of cuts and drains, held together by a fine cross-stitch of transparent thread. Drips, cannulas and tubes emerge through my skin as though the internal and the external have swapped places. I am an edifice of modern architecture. Inside, I float on the sound of rain. Outside, I heave in a web of plastic vessels full of my own bodily fluids. It hurts when I breathe, so I breathe gingerly, lightly, pretending not to, as though I am trying to deceive the pain.

A complicated graph at the end of my bed marks the lines for pressure and pulse, for temperature, for the quantities of piss and pus, and red and white blood cell counts. Every now and then someone comes to administer an injection and I am asked to give my name and my date of birth. I am not sure whether this is to check that I still know who I am, or that I am still me and not an impostor, as though anyone would want to swap places with me. A nurse comes to take a sample of my blood and can't quite decide where to insert another needle. So many of my arteries have needles sticking out of them already. I tell her that villagers in Serbia believe that injections and vaccinations given in the course of a lifetime prevent the deceased from turning into a vampire. I am safe from that threat at least. I try not to joke too often because it hurts when I laugh.

———

My husband and my son bring flowers and fresh fruit every day, leaving splashes of colour behind them in my grey hospital enclosure. When I can't sleep, I listen to the sound of non-existent rain pelting the windowpanes and try to remember the way my body looked when it was intact. It was only days ago but the memory is already fading. I am no longer sure what once lay in the place of the furrows of fresh scars trimmed with beads of bright red dew. In the black-and-white ultrasound photographs of my breasts, the most intimate pictures I've ever allowed anyone to take, the cancer cells are the bright, coloured spots. They cluster like purple grapes against the darkness of the healthy tissue. They are the only image of myself which I find impossible to forget.

I see a 23-year-old girl with wavy, dark hair, reading a chunky volume in the tall grass by the basketball courts on the Gypsy Island on the Sava river in Belgrade. From time to time, she stands up, stretches her arms and throws a ball or two with the boys. Her suntanned body is simultaneously muscular and plump. Her breasts are so firm that they barely move when she takes a jump upwards and then stands back, smiling, to follow the curve of the ball through the hoop. She wipes her brow with the back of her hand. 'Veki!' a young man calls the girl's name from one of the forlorn tables at a small waterside café. 'Drop that book and come over here. I've been watching you, kid. You've been reading the same page all day.' His blond hair is gathered in a ponytail. In the distance, Belgrade shimmers under a blanket of smog. The sky is still, cloudless. A swallow takes a long dive towards the water.

———

Through convalescence, I revisit the year before I met Simon again and again because it represented the last moment when everything could just as easily have turned out differently. I had won a scholarship for postgraduate study in France; I had an offer of a job at an American university (a lectureship in Serbo-Croat, small-time stuff, but the location on the edge of the Pacific appealed to my romantic instincts); I had a marriage proposal from Tomislav. The fact that I had considered all three options, but chosen none, appeals to my sense of destiny. Rather than confirm the idea of free will, as it should, the memory of myself standing at a crossroads paradoxically strengthens my conviction that everything is written for us in advance.

I see myself, just turned twenty-three, struggling to reach an ultimately irrelevant decision. I don't know what adventures now await me in this hospital bed in the cancer ward high above the roofs of west London. I don't even know whether the rain will ever stop. This is perhaps why I enjoy the certainty that the 23-year-old would be all right; that she would be happy beyond words, from the moment when she first embraced the young Englishman on an echoing corridor of the Karl Marx Institute in Sofia and for the two subsequent decades at least. Could anyone really ask for more?

I relive the long summer of 1984, allowing myself to be seduced, letting go, over and over again. Whatever happens now, I repeat to myself, the two of us have already proved to be more enduring than the world.

———

Then I begin to wonder whether the shadow has been there all along, like a scene painted by De Chirico. The Belgrade girl does not know it yet, but she will outlive the country she is leaving. The body she travels in so boldly will be cut and patched, and soon she will be able to seduce only in a different, much more haunting way. She will enchant the connoisseurs of suffering. 'How fetching is your garland of thorns!' her future lovers will have to say. 'How attractive that homemade look!' She can no more escape the world she is coming from – her flawed East

European self – than I can slip through the rain and out of the London hospital room.

Halfway through 1916, my grandfather sits somewhere in the darkness of south-eastern Poland by the swollen waters of a river whose name he doesn't know. At dawn, the clinking of Cossack swords, no louder than the sound of a spoon falling against the side of a china cup, announces that thousands are on the move. Grandfather shivers in his grey Habsburg tunic, listening out for the Russians, enemy-brothers.

I am scarred by the evaporation of the communist empire just as much as Grandpa was by the fall of the Habsburgs. He was twenty-four when the dual monarchy collapsed, I was twenty-eight when the crowds first danced on the wall in Berlin. He went over to the Russians, I went over to the English, in both cases before the outcome of the war was clear. I had grown up under the hammer-and-sickle banner, which, like the image of Christ, I can't quite get out of my bloodstream. My eyes were trained to look towards the beautiful Utopia, that first dawn of the Marxist not-yet. For that training, I love and despise and pity my educators.

I am often haunted by memories of the vanished socialist world. Uninvited fragments which float before my eyes manage to be vivid and melancholy at the same time. They have the strange quality of outtakes from a home movie which never seems to play at the correct speed. I see the trains emptying of picnickers at the border station of Villa Opicina, just to the east of Trieste, then filling again with grey people lugging the gaudy chattels of despair, freshly purchased in Italy, eastwards into Yugoslavia – the trinkets which we took home as symbols of a better life in better places. And further east, where not even the ornate plastic reached, hundreds of young women a bit less lucky but otherwise just like myself dutifully attended classes in schools named after Karl Marx and Friedrich Engels, wrote essays to mark the comrades' birth- and death-days, and learned to shoot, play music and speak foreign languages perfectly, with little hope of using them.

I once sat on a park bench in a small Ukrainian town just across the border from Hungary – a drab railway junction called Chop – watching a couple dance under a loudspeaker which, for reasons best known to the Soviet authorities, broadcast music into the forlorn, fly-blown summer afternoon. She was wearing a light red summer dress, a pair of snow-white socks and heavy, black boots with incongruous little heels. He had a pistachio-green suit with a tiny medal on the wide lapel. My father and mother came back from their walk with a glass of soda and pear syrup from one of the street dispensers. The couple were getting closer to each other, slowing down. I took a sip of soda when the music suddenly changed to an army march.

———

My generation and I thought that we could somehow avoid the pain. The promise was there in our education: a brighter tomorrow without a cloud, an expensive new dawn for which hundreds and thousands had laid down their lives in the Second World War. We had it all rammed into us: the gratitude for the carefree mornings paid for in advance by the comrades; plenitude in exchange for obedience. So long as we were thankful and toed the line, nothing could possibly go wrong.

When Comrade Tito died, he gave us back the keys to our castle. 'You can roam freely everywhere, but on no account open the door of this little room, whatever noises you hear coming from inside. See, this is the key and this is the lock, but you must never ever open the door. Do you understand, never ever?' said Comrade Tito, and left, hopping, on his one remaining leg.

For a long time, my English voice sounded quite unlike my Serbian one, in a way which irritated me. The more insecure I felt, the more emptily correct my language became. The shards of memory, of everything that there was before I came to London, were embedded so firmly into Serbian that they wouldn't translate without pain.

Then illness and fear made the memories erupt. For better or worse, English had to do. Where I was once happy in not belonging, I now wanted to be all in one place just as much as I needed to be all in one piece. I longed for shelter and protection. I no longer wanted any prizes, other than my son's continuing knowledge of me. Once that is accomplished, I can drink wine and listen to music and watch the wind dance in the crowns of trees. Or die; whichever it happens to be.

I brought Simon to Belgrade to meet my parents in the spring of 1985. Roughly at the same time, my friend Olya – a poet who wrote sophisticated verse which secretly made me feel quite jealous – was having an affair with a young German student from Freiburg. They translated large chunks of Georg Trakl's poetry into Serbian and spent long, passionate weekends in various cathedral towns in Alsace. The budding generation of Belgrade princesses was obviously becoming very cosmopolitan just then. 'At least Vesna is seeing an Englishman,' Olya's mother commented. The hierarchy of nationalities, arranged according to a vague order of desirability, as seen through the lenses of our cosy, still-enclosed world, soon became practically the only topic I was allowed to discuss as I moved from one Belgrade coffee party to another. Simon smiled beatifically and ate elaborate *petits fours* under the watchful eyes of dozens of versions of his future mother-in-law, to the manner born.

Our discussions often resembled those old jokes about 'an Englishman, a Frenchman and a Serb' in which the Serbs generally came off best. They were ours, and 'ours' in this context – for better or worse – does not really translate into English. There was an implicit consensus that marrying a fellow Serb would have been better for me, more 'natural', as though I was marrying outside the species. This was somewhat mitigated by the fact that Simon was so obviously a well-educated young man with the kind of family background that no one could complain much about, try as they might. And they did try. Who was good enough for their girl, after all? To rubber-stamp her choice would be bad manners.

———

If the Serbs tended to come off best in the story of 'an Englishman, a Frenchman and a Serb', I am afraid that the Frenchmen generally won the second place. For an average Serbian lady of middle-class persuasion (communist or not), the French were clearly the 'if you must marry a foreigner' bridegrooms of choice. While other nationalities attracted a host of different prejudices, the French, and the Parisians in particular, had a kind of Teflon image to which nothing bad ever seemed to stick. That brand of non empirical Francophilia was ubiquitous in the Balkans. Everything that was wrong with Yugoslavia was reliably just right in France. The French were handsome, courteous, elegant, admirers of fine art and fine foods, passionate lovers best epitomized by characters in novels such as *La Dame aux Camélias*.

In short, they somehow managed to preserve the kind of image which might have been designed by a joint committee of the French Tourist Board and the French Ministry of Culture at the height of the Belle Epoque. Even during the bombing of

Serbia in 1999, many of my female relations managed to hate the Americans, the English and the Germans (especially the Germans!), but found it in their hearts to excuse the French. 'They didn't really want this! The Americans made them do it,' said one of them. She was horribly upset at the fact that the monument to Franco-Serbian friendship in the Kalemegdan Park was draped in a black cloth intended to cover the engraved verse urging the Serbian nation to 'love France as she has loved us', not even beginning to see that just then this might have sounded ironic.

I once became involved in what the French so appropriately call *une amitié amoureuse* over a few weeks in Paris. I was nineteen. At thirty-one, Henri seemed to me thrillingly ancient. He was actually born in the forties (in October 1949, to be absolutely precise), and was a student of literature at the Sorbonne in May 1968: a walking piece of French history as far as I was concerned. He was a teacher at a Parisian *lycée*, an aspiring theatre director, a communist and a lover of poetry. We met in a bookshop on Rue Monsieur Le Prince one dark afternoon, and continued our conversation through a long, rainy evening in a nearby café.

Henri lived on one of the quieter streets of the seventh arrondissement, in a maid's room connected via a balcony door to the much grander flat in which his mother and father, both in their seventies, sat at a table of polished mahogany, endlessly bent over crossword puzzles from *Le Figaro*. They were watched by ancestral portraits of dour-looking civil servants of the Republic, a collection of upright men who could easily have played the deceived husbands in any one of the big nineteenth-century French novels of adultery.

Henri's mother offered a cold, bony hand with a couple of extraordinarily large rings. 'Enchanted to meet a little friend of my son's,' she said politely. Both she and her husband seemed to be a good ten inches shorter and infinitely thinner than I was, which – given my pretty average height and weight – was probably incorrect, but it went some way towards explaining why Henri was barely taller than me and so thin that he seemed to cross his legs in at least three places when he sat down. I was the Slav Gulliver in a French Lilliput, a Russian woman lieu-tenant entering Berlin, flagpole in one hand, grenade in the other, a tight *rubashka* over big, bouncy bosoms. 'Belgrade, did you say?' Henri's mother looked up towards me. 'Our cleaning lady is from —' and she named a village some 150 miles south of Belgrade.

The same story repeated itself again and again over the ensuing days. Every time I met a friend or relation of Henri's, I'd hear about a lovely nurse, a manicurist, a car mechanic or a little woman in the bakery to whom I was connected by virtue of nationality. My exotic value in Paris was precisely nil. That, I hasten to add, was probably not the reason why my relationship with Henri remained *une amitié* rather than turning into *une affaire*. He was very generous and impeccably polite, and even attractive in a sort of dishevelled, just-awakened, boyish way. Nonetheless, I realized that I would never be able to love a man who could not carry me under one arm while holding a machine-gun or lassoing a steer with the other. So much for feminism and the love of poetry and philosophy. I put it down to survival instincts bred deep into my genes during long centuries of near slavery in the Ottoman Empire.

Henri clearly enjoyed playing Professeur Higgins to my Slav Eliza Doolittle. In a matter of weeks, my elisions became near perfect. I wasn't a dustman's daughter but, nonetheless, there were so many things I hadn't tried at that stage: cheeses, wines, savoury water-ices, French poetry beyond Aragon, avant-garde theatre, galleries without tourists. French men as well, but Henri and I never really progressed beyond flirtatious conversational hints, which themselves improved my French vocabulary.

I might have been too young or, now I sometimes suspect, remembering nothing more specific than a gesture, there might have been another man somewhere in the equation, a French Colonel Pickering, hidden from view. In all probability, things would not have turned out very differently if that were so. I only register it to say that, according to the received wisdom of Belgrade's Francophile ladies, the Frenchmen were never inclined that way, no sirree! English gentlemen, however, as products of their famously all-male educational system were...
au contraire.

———

If every Parisian I met seemed to have had dealings of one kind or another with at least two Serbs, the London I finally settled in was refreshingly free of such connections. My father-in-law dimly remembered a member of the Serbian royal family from his Eton days, and quickly latched on to the martial glories of Montenegro; my grandmother-in-law, remembering two world wars, simply thought of Serbs as very brave; and my mother-in-law knew a Slovene daffodil farmer in Cornwall. Most of the people I met knew where Yugoslavia was and many had travelled through it for one reason or another, so there was no need for long explanations when I said where I was from. At the same time, and until the waves of refugees reached British shores in the 1990s, most tended to have no acquaintances among my compatriots, and, for better or worse, few illusions or prejudices other than those Occidentals then commonly harboured towards East Europeans.

Back in Belgrade, however, my forthcoming marriage and the distinct chance that I might soon be giving birth to little English people (with everything that implied) brought to the surface a veritable hotchpotch of ideas of Englishness, most of them mildly or not so mildly negative. Most Serbs I knew used the word English to mean British, so there was no let-off for the Welsh or the Scots either. Thus, for example:

The English were perfidious and treacherous. Winston Churchill supported the royalist resistance in 1941 only to dump the entire Serbian nation unceremoniously into the hands of the commies without a second thought. This reflected the fact that the English had never been our true friends but had always simply used us in whatever was the great power deal of the day.

The English were, on the whole, ugly. For every British-born Cary Grant and every Vivien Leigh there were literally hundreds who looked downright weird. Belgrade television, with its endless repeats of programmes such as *The Benny Hill Show*, *Are You Being Served?* and *Hi-de-hi*, did not help. Neither did the fact that members of the royal family were somehow thought of as 'typically English'.

The English were either arrogant, cold aristocrats or boorish, beer-drinking football hooligans. The latter 'needed a war, badly, to get the violence out of their system', according to my practical grandmother.

England had, quite possibly, the worst climate in the world. The entire history of England could be viewed as a series of attempts to escape the weather. The English climate was likely to make me suicidal sooner or later. A neighbour turned up with a copy of *Wuthering Heights*, in which she had highlighted some pertinent descriptions of rain for my delectation.

English sex was an oxymoron. We were too polite to discuss this, but there were hints that English couples were supposed to sleep in separate bedrooms after the birth of their children. In Montenegro, there was a story – perhaps an urban or, rather, a very rural myth, I am not sure – that the mother-in law sometimes slept (in the most innocent sense) with her future daughter-in-law to check whether her feet were warm and thus ensure that she would make a worthwhile bedfellow for the son during the long winter nights. As an English bride, my blood circulation was obviously irrelevant I should need to keep no one warm but myself.

England had perhaps the strangest cuisine in the world. They were reputed to have developed a special jam for every kind of meat, and they smothered their lamb with mint and vinegar. (This made Granny laugh, for Montenegrins are connoisseurs of fine lamb.) The English did not know what to do with vegetables, other than roots, as could be expected of northerners. 'And God only knows what their patisserie is like,' worried one aunt, while everyone tried hard to remember an English kind of cake.

Simon's paternal grandfather: l'Angleterre profonde

'Reform Torte,' said a neighbour, referring to a fine confection of praline and walnut sponge, but no one was convinced that it was English. We imagined medieval bricks of dough which had to be soaked in milky tea. When Simon sat down to eat, Granny kept wondering whether any of the jars of jam from the larder – plum, rosehip, greengage, strawberry, melon – should be brought out to accompany his main course.

Simon's paternal grandmother

In fact, anything Simon did, any time, anywhere, was examined as an example of 'what the English do'. He was not so much himself as a photo-fit for different aspects of Englishness. On a Danube pleasure cruise, two people came up to me to enquire about my travelling companion. 'I knew from his shoes that he was English the moment I saw him,' remarked a plump Yugoslav diplomat. 'Is it true that they are very cold?' asked a woman in a tight silk dress with a corsage of peonies, smiling broadly towards Simon in a vain attempt to obscure the line her enquiry was taking. He smiled back and muttered something about 'the lady's very fine pencil moustache'. I was, for perhaps the millionth time in my life, engaged in creative interpreting. Others patted his shoulder more benevolently, repeating, '*Srpski zet!*' ('Serbian son-in-law') as though he were somehow marrying the whole nation. In a sense, he was. '*Da, da,*' Simon replied in an impressive show of Serbo-Croat fluency.

———

These were not the only worries about the fate which awaited me in England. Even if it all worked out perfectly, marriage-wise, what was I going to do there? Women in my family have been working since time began and staying at home was not an option anyone considered seriously. I was endlessly told the same story of the novelist Milos Tsernianski – the temporary tenant of Lady Paget's coach house in Kingston. In his London exile, Tsernianski could only find work as a book-keeper in a shoeshop in Bond Street. Fears of failure, or perhaps of the inability to transplant success, so often seemed to scar the Yugoslav perspectives of the outside world. My conviction that everything would work out was seen as evidence of nothing but my youth and inexperience. No one said it, but the question was implicit in every example of greatness unrecognized which was thrown in my direction: What hope was there for me?

———

During my hospital stay, my mother-in-law rang the ward every day. Her care was both attentive and completely different from my mother's, perhaps because I didn't feel any need to shield her from bad news. She sent cards and letters and parcels of bright, airy clothes which were intended to cheer me up: African kaftans, Pakistani *shalwar kamiz* and dozens of big scarves for turbans (cotton, because silk slides off a bald head), Tuareg necklaces and bracelets, large silver earrings, detective stories, memoirs, pictures of rolling English hills, brochures of country houses to rent when I was well again. She didn't, even for a moment, allow for the possibility that I wouldn't be.

A history graduate from Westfield College in London, my mother-in-law blazed the trail as a trendy left-wing Goldsworthy bride in the sixties. She campaigned against my cancer just as she had campaigned while the Yugoslav war was raging. She wrote letters to MPs, to the Prime Minister, to God, for all I knew, explaining the ins and outs of the Balkan crisis to anyone who cared to listen. I am not sure if our different ways of battling against suffering – for I see no great difference in the degree of courage – say something about our different origins. I harden and travel inwards, where the pain can't reach me; she engages with every weapon at her disposal. She believes that she, alone, can make a difference in a way in which I never could.

———

When the biopsy needle went into my right breast, I knew the truth. Like a diver emerging from the dark waters with heavy metal lungs, the needle drew out its haul of poisoned cells. The surgeon, a woman of my age with straight glossy hair and bright dark eyes, followed her training in delivering bad news. No lies, no promises, no false dawns, but no fear either: 'Yes, I am afraid it doesn't look good.' I was the first to utter the c-word. I asked, 'Why me?' as I suppose everyone does. Suddenly, every other destiny seemed preferable. She had no answer. Indeed, it could have been her. A year later, we were friends.

———

A nurse wearing civilian clothes (the special corps of cancer troops) took me aside to a hospital room which was obviously meant to be more like home, furnished with a comfortable sofa, a vase of flowers and two boxes of tissues at the ready, a world away from the hard plastic chairs and linoleum in the corridor outside. It felt as unreal as an undertaker's office or a morning-TV studio. I sat on the sofa and took a tissue, and then froze. I couldn't quite decide whether to be brave or start sobbing on the nurse's shoulder. She had seen us all before: the jokers, the stiff upper lippers, the tragedians. I only had this one take. 'I am sorry, Michelle. I don't seem to have any questions. I should really be going home now.' I stood up, walked towards the door, then turned back. 'How am I going to tell my parents?' I asked, as though I had broken the most important promise I'd ever given them.

———

I knew how I was going to tell or not tell Simon. He was waiting for the phone to ring: a wordless call would suffice. That morning, I asked him not to come with me to the hospital, just as I asked him to stay away from the maternity ward almost three years before to the day, when our son was born. This was not always an easy thing to do in a world which assumed that his duty was to be by my side, but he didn't mind. He understood that I was made of different mettle. I faced both my demons and my gods alone.

I walked out of the hospital slowly. The sounds of the city were muffled and distant. The day seemed to have been created for bad news. I stared at the familiar bends of the river. I could walk like this for ever, but I was scared of returning home on my own. Finally I called Simon to ask him to meet me. His tall, familiar figure emerged from the mist of a dying February afternoon. 'A widower,' I thought, almost as though I was checking the word out for size. We tried intermittently to say something, but it was difficult to know where to start. I kept apologizing. I felt that I had betrayed him too in some way, worse than ever before.

I kept thinking that I was being punished for having it all so easy in the past. This was ridiculous, given that I believed in neither karmic destiny nor hubris, but how is a dialectical materialist supposed to face terminal illness? My luck simply had to run out at some stage, I figured, and wished it had run out differently. I tried to be realistic. Even if it all ended tomorrow, no one except my mother could really say that I died young at forty-one.

I told myself I wasn't frightened, but I kept waking up at three a.m. drenched in sweat, staring death in the face. I thought about Alexander's future, and tried to be falsely generous towards Simon, thinking that he would remarry and forget, but I clearly wanted neither. I wanted to know for certain that he would spend the rest of his days sobbing at my grave and that no one would ever be able to replace me.

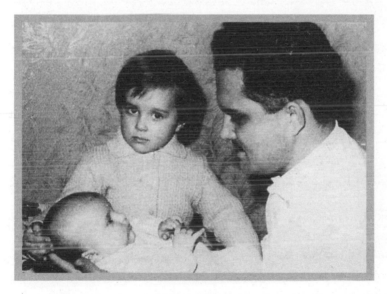

With my baby sister

A week later it became much worse. One of the scans showed that the cancer had spread to my bones. We needed a repeat before we could be sure, but meanwhile the hospital vocabulary had changed, just in case. We talked about palliative care, maintenance, a positive attitude. No one mentioned *treatment* any longer. The grim reaper seemed to be sharpening his scythe. I kept being either cheerfully sarcastic or angry. I suspected that my positive attitude was somehow meant to make things easier for everyone else, and I rebelled in small, childish ways. One day, I was barely able to function at the thought of my own end, while the next I had become so accustomed to it that I was able to stop off and buy myself a sandwich at a riverside bar as I walked home from the hospital along the Thames. The river's tides were strangely comforting. 'The world will just go on without me,' I thought as I munched tuna on wholemeal bread and drank carrot juice, and contemplated the uselessness of my healthy eating habits. I had, self-evidently, not a single original thought about death.

———

Two weeks on and I gave up on the idea that I'd ever sleep past three a.m. again. Instead, I got up, put on my dressing gown and tried, pathetically, to get on with my academic writing. I was halfway through a book on travel when the world as I knew it ended. I had never noticed it before, but the newspapers were full of heroic examples of people who had climbed Everest in metastasis. Hitting the keyboard with my two index fingers seemed comparatively easy.

It wasn't going anywhere. I'd get up from my desk and walk to the bathroom and look at myself in the mirror, porcelain pale and poisoned. I stood on the tiles, feeling that I was like one of those shiny apples which you bite into, only to spit out brown, rotten flesh. I couldn't decide whether that was the legacy of my East European youth – all those factory chimneys belching black sulphurous smoke, all those coal fires – or of my Western European life – the plastic gloss on everything, invisible, equally poisoned. I needed to pin the blame somewhere. I needed to feel really angry. I couldn't.

One morning at four a.m., I gave up on my travel book and started writing a 'life-without-Vesna' manual for Simon. This was meant to be a practical little booklet, no tears, no deathbed speeches. He and I had – in the many years of living together – developed a system of duty-sharing, running the home in the fashion of German U-boat crews. No talk, no detectable traces.

I did my work and he did his; what one knew the other need not worry about. I now set out to write down my portion of the U-boat duty rota. I listed my bank accounts and the bills I settled each month, my pitiful pension schemes and my savings funds: life's administrative debris. Then I wrote down how to set the video recorder and the washing machine, and how to program each of a surprising number of timers around the house. The more pointless the instructions seemed, the happier I felt writing them out.

My own choices seemed to funnel rapidly. I enjoyed the feeling of being in control, perhaps because control was the last thing I really had. Even the 'life manual' was getting out of hand. If it became longer than 3,000 words it would be as good as useless, the teacher in me worried. Then I realized that the reason I enjoyed writing it was the passwords to the past which I kept burying in the text. I was floating messages in a bottle which would mean nothing to anybody else except the two of us.

My son, on the other hand, was too young to have such shared memories. Only two at the time of my diagnosis, he would, in all likelihood, have difficulty remembering me in a couple of years' time. My photographs would erase my living face. The world I came from would seem as exotic and distant to him as accounts of nineteenth-century explorations of the source of the Nile.

I was aware that although, since their late-Victorian heyday, his English ancestors kept moving into smaller and smaller dwellings, much of their history was still around. It was all there for Alexander to touch and see: the paintings, commissions signed by Victoria and George, letters of love and business, and pieces of uniform and dress.

His Serbian blood was, by comparison, like an underground river. The drifts of Balkan life meant that we kept little in writing, and sold or lost most that was of value from the past. We started afresh at regular intervals and owned barely anything that was older than us. I distilled everything further when I came to England: down to four suitcases, of which two were filled with books. I was so uninterested in material possessions that joining a family where everything was already in place was a blessing. The thought of decorating and furnishing a house – the kind of thing my mother loved – bored me. I was happy simply to move in. Now I wanted to write myself into the picture in a way which surprised me. I was trying to capture my voice for Alexander so that he could hear it if and when he wanted to. His Serbian was poor and that was my fault, for I had always spoken English to him. Now my English – such as it was – would have to serve a sacred duty. I put the 'life manual' to one side and began to write my life for Alexander.

———

A week later, the second scan showed that the cancer was still *in situ* and hadn't spread. Everyone was talking about treatment again. It would be removed, counter-poisoned with the finest pharmaceuticals, you will sail through. Fear not, girl. Overwhelmingly – 76 per cent, according to statistics – the chances are that you will still be around five years from now. You are so strong, it is probably more than 76 anyway. I no longer really cared. I was, of course, glad to hear the good news, but my happiness had, in the meantime, ceased to depend on scan results. The illness had articulated the odds which everyone faced sooner or later. 'Why me?' somehow translated into 'Why not?' For whatever reason, I simply didn't fear death any more.

———

'Come on, hit me if you like,' I said. Death stared at me for a long moment. I stared back.

———

The false starts, the dislocations, the fractures, the stitches, the leitmotifs of arrival and departure: I am at peace with everything that I once took as a sign of my weakness. The thirst for new experiences managed to keep me dreaming of adventures even when I thought I was dying. 'Had I only stayed there, I would have been this or that by now,' I used to say when I was unhappy with the hand of cards I held, knowing full well that I never really wanted to stay *there*, whatever that meant at any given moment. When I was pinned down by pain and plastic tubes on a hospital bed, while it rained so hard that I didn't wish to leave anyway, I turned back, perhaps for the first time, and stared into the picture I drew by my restlessness.

In its fragmented way, my life makes perfect sense. There is nothing extraordinary about it, but, as I try to write it down, I can feel it burning. I hear the flicker of its flames as distinctly as I once heard the sound of Alexander's heart in my womb; as clearly as I heard the sound of blood pulsating in the transplanted artery in the transplanted flesh which now represents a large portion of my breast; the sound of fresh beginnings. My body, strangely, now seems all the more beautiful to me for the way it is mapped by scars, like a cracked but unbroken vessel. I sleep well past three in the morning again, but I take nothing for granted any more.

AFTERWORD

None of the people or places I refer to in this memoir is invented, although a few of the personal names are, mainly in those cases where I was in no position to check whether someone would mind being included in my life story, or where I was and was told that they wanted their identity disguised. I have also taken the liberty of combining one or two minor personalities, in a way which I hope simplifies things but which is of no consequence to the story of my life, such as it is. I don't wish to hurt anyone.

For most of my readers, the pages of this book will contain names of people and places which may appear difficult and alien. I decided to follow the example of those old Balkan travel books I love by transcribing names into English wherever practical, rather than always using the diacritics from the

Serbo-Croatian version of the Latin alphabet, as is now common practice. This is not an ideal solution, but it is the one which appealed to me the most. It may upset the purists, but, as I suggested somewhere in this book, proper names – including my own – are not something I argue about with anyone.

The most interesting insights I have had while writing this memoir relate to the ways in which individual memory works. It connects people and places and things which may superficially seem unconnected, and imposes its own patterns across time. To have written a linear narrative of my life – from birth to the present – would have been to force my story to acquire a shape which it doesn't have in the way I remember it, and to jettison those very patterns and leitmotifs which seem to me the most interesting. I would have to leave the end blank for another hand to write that death scene which I will never be able to describe. I refer to the many possible beginnings in the opening chapter, but I am aware of the ways in which the ending changes the meaning of the entire story. A memoir can only be written from a slowly shifting vantage point in the flow of the experience it describes. Its meaning is at best makeshift.

Regardless of whether its author realizes it or not, an auto-biography is a doubly edited life. Memory edits the first run, the writer edits the second, as she imposes provisional boundaries on her recollection. In this book I wrote about my and my family's past as I remember it. I chose not to revisit my adolescent diaries, which are both patchy and stored in a house at the other end of the continent, nor my adult appointment diaries, which could remind me of too many insignificant things. I didn't want to research anything. I did little to compare notes even with those who are closest to me. This is not a faithful reconstruction of the past; it is an imprint of individual memory. If there are factual errors, and I am sure there are, it is because I remember things wrongly. That seems interesting too.

London, 27 July 2004

ACKNOWLEDGEMENTS

My agent, Faith Evans, my editor, Clara Farmer, and others at Atlantic Books, and my childhood friend Zana Kovincic, who spared time from her duties in the Peruvian diplomatic service, have all helped in different ways to make this book more beautiful. John Nicoll's advice was, as always, very valuable.

My sister, Vera Dodic, used a hard-earned break from her busy Toronto office to sift patiently through countless shoeboxes of family photographs under the watchful and sometimes tearful eyes of my parents in Belgrade. As so many times before, she had the difficult task of explaining what exactly I was up to. I am sorry I could not be there to help.

In addition to the members of my family who took most of the photographs in this book, and in particular my uncle-in-law Douglas Goldsworthy, I must thank Dejan Corovic, who took the photograph on the front cover many more years ago than I care to remember.

My husband, Simon, was always there to help and – although he is a reserved and private man – understood why I needed to tell this story. My son, Alexander, kindly lent me what he maintains to be his computer to enable me to write it. My love and my profound gratitude to them – and to my parents, Milos and Nada Bjelogrlic – is, I hope, apparent in this memoir.

My thanks go to the many doctors and nurses who, in an unusually literal sense, made this book possible: my family doctor, Dr Venkatesham; and, at Charing Cross Hospital, Professor Charles Coombes, Dr David Vigushin, Dr Charles Lowdell and Dr Simon Wood; Vanessa Cross, Ann Alexander and all the other nurses who were there when I needed them most, to laugh at my jokes, admire my wigs and turbans, and make sure that the needles didn't hurt.

My fondest thanks are reserved for my surgeon, Jacqueline Lewis. Her dedication, warmth and friendship made me happy to be alive even when it seemed terribly hard work. I still can't think of many things which are as wonderful as waking up from the anaesthetic after seven hours of surgery to see Jackie's smiling face.

EPILOGUE TO THE
PAPERBACK EDITION

Life after *Strawberries*

Chernobyl Strawberries grew out of poisoned soil, yet, from its beginnings, this book has been nothing but a happy project for me. In the seventeen months of its writing – between February 2003 and July 2004, while I was undergoing treatment for cancer – its creation felt just as healing as the offerings of conventional medicine. It proved to be the most effective of painkillers, for it managed not only to make me forget the pain, but also to make time pass more quickly, which is rather more than the usual pills can do.

We see things not as they are, but as we are, says one of the holy books, I forget which. I wouldn't wish those months in the Tropic of Cancer on my worst enemy, but I wouldn't give them back either. I hated the pain so much that it took a while to see that cancer gave me certain things too, including the luxurious gift of this book. I wouldn't have written it but for the possibility that time might be running out.

I penned chunks of it on my walks around the hospital ward, scribbling on scraps of paper and in small notebooks tucked into the same canvas bag which concealed drainage bottles, my blood and words together. No one batted an eyelid at my literary antics. In the big West London teaching hospital where I was treated, the nurses had seen it all before. Two of the people on my ward were recovering from gender realignment surgery. Late at night I could hear them through the rows of curtains separating our beds, whispering to each other in counter-tenor. Even that didn't seem strange. Some patients were losing their breasts, others gaining new ones; some were happy to be starting different lives, others simply to be alive.

I brooded over images of my childhood and adolescence in Belgrade in the cold twilight of radiotherapy rooms. My past seemed suspended in the sun-encased memory but was clearly visible, like an insect in amber. At home, writing always demanded the luxury of a clear desk and a clear day, and I felt lucky when I stole one of those in a month. I wrote painstakingly and slowly. Sometimes I complained by e-mail to a friend who lives on a ranch in Oregon, when we were both awake in front of our computer screens at different ends of the night and in different time zones, a world away from London in every sense. She has authored many books and I hoped to hear from her the secret of writing against the noise and through the distractions. There was none. 'Did you know that Nabokov used to lock himself in the bathroom, manuscript in his lap, while Vera and Dimitri played in their tiny Parisian flat?' she responded. Although I enjoyed writing, I hadn't felt that kind of overriding drive since I was a poetry-writing adolescent. Perhaps I was simply not meant to be a writer, I had decided. It didn't matter too much, but it didn't sound quite right.

On the ward, and for the first time since the poetic toil of my adolescence, I felt the same urge to cover blank sheets of paper with words, an urge strong enough to shut everything else away. I wrote while the moans of other patients, the hissing of TV sets and the smells of illness washed around me. Like Walter Benjamin's Angel of History, I could hurtle into the future but only with my eyes fixed firmly on the past. Far from the libraries and books and all the crutches I had tended to use in my writing before, I felt free to play with the shadows my life was throwing against the hospital wall. A book grew slowly in the crevasses between history and story. It was a wild, hybrid fruit of that deeper knowledge of myself for which I had no choice but to surrender a pound of flesh.

———

What I was trying to write was not a book about cancer. I often joked that I hardly wished myself to be remembered as 'the English patient' and I still don't. I wanted it to be a book about London and Belgrade, about the Serbian and English families to which I belong. While my body was cut and reconstructed, I was recreating a life story which seemed to me both very ordinary and unique. I found the uniqueness not so much where one most expects it – in the fulfilment of particular ambitions – but in the thirst with which I continued to take on the new. Such discoveries are perhaps the unexpected but beautiful fruit of writing things down in this way.

Still uncertain about what exactly to call my memoir, I played with different titles which connected my two divided worlds. I tried to join up the Danube and the Thames, Britain and Yugoslavia, the North West and the South East of Europe, but none of the options I came up with seemed to capture the sum of the book's parts. *Chernobyl Strawberries* had been there in the first sentence all along, and it offered a useful metaphor for the bittersweet Eastern European world I came from. The pollution of Chernobyl was not that different from the invisible ideological pollution amid which I grew up. At the same time, I knew that the world of my childhood had its allure too. I remembered the vulnerable, uncherished splendours behind the grey facades, and I felt a strange sort of obligation towards that memory.

By choosing to write in English, I was recreating that world in a new medium. The act of implicit translation – the carrying through of experience from one language into another – was something of which I was deeply aware, even when no-one else seems to have found the fact that I was writing this book in English particularly unusual. Were an Englishwoman to arrive in Belgrade with Serbian, picked up at twice-weekly lessons back at school, as her third language, and to find

295

herself a few years later teaching nineteenth-century Serbian literature to Serbian students at a Serbian university, and were she to write
a memoir in Serbian which is then translated back into English by
someone else... well, such a reverse scenario is almost too improbable to contemplate. However, my British compatriots are so used to
appropriations of their language to take much notice of acts of derring-
do (or foolishness) like mine; in fact, they sometimes seem to expect
nothing less.

The manuscript found its English publisher when it was barely half-
written and, soon afterwards, German and Serbian publishers too.
Although my first book was also originally written in English and translated into four different languages, it was an academic study and the
exchanges with translators were never this amusing. 'What kind of
shoe precisely is this brogue your father-in-law wore in Belgrade twenty
years ago?', my German translator asked from some Greek island
where she was working on my book. I scanned a picture and e-mailed
it back to Greece.

In her turn, my Serbian translator sent electronic mail from the
Illinois university where she was working on her PhD, and I forwarded
it from London to the publishing house in Belgrade. Seeing the little
literary world I created in English transported back into my native

tongue was in many ways an unsettling experience. I realised that I was originally able to write the book only by locking myself into English with the pretence that my parents and my friends would not read it. The book was a work of love, in every sense. I wasn't so much worried about its contents as strangely shy.

I also learned a lot about my own linguistic mannerisms in the process. If the translator chose a word I wouldn't have used — sometimes simply because she was twenty years younger and my mother tongue had changed in my absence – what I heard as a false note bothered me even when it was superficially more elegant. On one or two occasions, without even realising it, she translated the words from Serbian songs I had woven into the English narrative back to me, in an amusing version of Chinese whispers. Eventually, I relaxed. I stopped looking over her shoulder and let her get on with her work. Many years ago I translated a novel by Bruce Chatwin into Serbian, and I reminded myself that – had Bruce been able to interfere in my choice of Serbian synonyms – the work would have lost much of its charm. In fact, I never wanted to translate this book myself, partly because I was too busy enjoying myself in the afterglow of its English publication to rush back to my study, partly because I feared that I might end up writing a different book, wanting to explain and describe very different things. In Serbian, my memoir could become a book about England just as much as my English book is about Serbia.

Finally the translation was ready and I flew to Belgrade to open the Book Fair. The opening day is one of the high points of the season, and – as this was the fiftieth anniversary of the Fair's existence – it felt even more festive than usual. The opening ceremony was broadcast in direct transmission on the main TV channel and picked up in every news bulletin that evening. The Serbia I was returning to is a different country from the Yugoslavia I left twenty years ago. This event was truly live.

I had prepared two versions of a short speech, in Serbian and in English, uncertain which was more appropriate for the occasion. Every year, one country is chosen as the guest of honour and its writers are invited to special events such as this. I was flying back to Belgrade as a British writer, and – the organisers advised – it was more appropriate to deliver my speech in English, as a courtesy to the many English guests. When the reflector lights went up, I saw my parents' heads – now, unmistakably, brightly white – in the audience. I started reading the speech I knew they wouldn't understand. At least, this time, they had heard what their daughter was going to say in advance.

———

If the writing kept me going while I was in hospital, the production of the book and the aftermath of its publication helped when I was uncertain about how to step back into my day-to-day life. As I searched through my small collection of family photographs and trinkets for suitable illustrations, as I responded to editorial queries (easy, once I decided that the only point of reference required was myself), I was also – by being able to call this work – delaying the return to my 'civilian life'.

In fact, although it took me a while to recognise this, I faced the challenges war veterans must face after an armistice. The things I've learned at the hospital front-line made my old duties seem mundane, but they had, and still have, to be attended to. The lectures I prepare, the hundreds of student essays I mark every semester, the hours of travel to and from work on crowded trains and buses, the household tasks, the to-do lists which never seem to get any shorter, the bills and letters which always shout 'urgent!' at you: I now face them all again just as I had to face illness the year before. Nonetheless, while everything else may be flowing back into place like the water closing over a sunken vessel, life after *Strawberries* is perceptibly different, and that difference makes the quotidian much easier to take on.

Even before it came out, I had decided to throw myself into everything good that this book may bring, to live it and enjoy it to the full, just in case I never managed to complete another one. Such is the superstitious wisdom of the battle-scarred. The extent and the sheer joy of it all took me by surprise. I dreamed of one or two good reviews in my favourite little literary magazines, but not of serialization in *The Times* and on the BBC, nor of the press cuttings which started to arrive almost every day from different corners of Europe. I can't pretend I didn't enjoy it. Having been through so much that I wanted to forget I was now given an abundance of memories to treasure.

As I write this, less than eight months after its publication, the memoir has been on bestseller lists in four different countries, a rare thing for a life story of someone as unknown as me. Amazingly, it has had over three hundred reviews. The number of words others have written about this book is already much greater than the number of words I wrote inside it. Could one feel anything but flattered? I gradually lost the sense of myself as an academic interloper and began to feel at home in the writing business. At literary festivals, I met authors whose work I have read and taught for many years and, while I resisted the urge to cross-examine them on my students' behalf, I watched carefully and learned. Finally, but perhaps most importantly, I now count a number of those readers who have written to me or attended one of my events among my friends. In that, I see a reassuring balance of effort and outcome which is in itself a rare gift from fate.

We often mistakenly assume that laughter and beauty are mutually exclusive; while I was writing *Chernobyl Strawberries*, I kept saying that the book I wanted to produce was the kind I fall in love with myself, one that is not afraid to be funny and poetic at the same time. I thought that my readers would turn out to be very similar to me, and I was not mistaken. In fact, the sheer wealth of encounters this book has brought – in person or through the letters and e-mails I received – represented its most unexpected consequence. I told the story of my life and I received other stories in return. Many offered personal histories of displacement. The world is full of refugees and children of refugees, and, just like me, many of my readers were people whose notions of home can only ever be multiple and whose accent, like mine, means that they might be asked 'how long are you staying for?' even when it has been more than half a lifetime.

Migration was far from being the dominant theme of the letters I received. My readers wrote of illnesses and miracle cures, of falling in love, of career changes and precious late children, of youthful poetry lived for then abandoned, or simply of their favourite books. What I think of as my most courageous steps – moving from one end of the continent to the other at the call of youthful love, learning to live in another language, or facing death and finding that I am not afraid of it – are acts of ordinary courage after all.

I sometimes wonder whether I would have received the same numbers and the same kinds of letters had I instead written a novel or a collection of essays. These forms have often been employed to tell a story which is essentially autobiographical. Although I could see distinct advantages in those genres in which everything ends exactly the way one wants when I began to write this book they seemed an option for those who had the luxury of time. The fact that I am now working on a novel – very, very slowly – is a reflection both of a renewed sense that I might have enough time for luxuries after all, and of the sheer enjoyment of creating fiction. And, although nothing is certain, I am glad that *Chernobyl Strawberries* may yet turn out to be a step on a writing path rather than its conclusion. I often joke that I enjoy my 'posthumous life' more than the one I lived before. The fact that a memoir has come to represent a beginning rather than a summing up, appeals to my sense of a life in which so many things have been topsy-turvy.

The challenge I set myself was to write a story which was not linear yet which nonetheless managed to make the reader want to know what happened later, to read on with a sense of curiosity and, if possible, even urgency. Obviously, as is implicit in the memoir as a genre, the heroine does not die – not just yet – but does she live happily ever after? Yes, yes, dear reader, she lives a happy 'after'. About 'ever', let's wait and see.

Vesna Goldsworthy,
London, December 2005.

302

My eleven favourite books

Last spring, I was asked to list my favourite books for a literary festival. I found the idea frustrating and kept wanting to change the line-up even when the orders for a special display were dispatched. As soon as I listed my choices, I realised that I had offered eleven rather than the customary ten titles, but couldn't bear to delete one simply for the sake of decimal conventions. I have to admit that I love nothing so much as spying around other people's shelves to check which books are well thumbed and which are still suspiciously pristine. I never feel fully at ease in houses in which the books are hidden or absent. 'Tell me what you read, and I'll tell you who you are' is something I really believe in.

Dates shown indicate the year of first publication.

1. Leo Tolstoy, *Anna Karenina* (1877)

When I was a student in Belgrade, in our (often very pretentious) bookish circles the question 'Tolstoy or Dostoevsky?' was the literary equivalent of 'The Beatles or the Stones?'. We tended to choose Dostoevsky (and the Stones). At twenty, he somehow seemed more profound, more earth-shattering than Tolstoy. When I returned to *Anna Karenina* in my late thirties, I was bewitched by the complexities of marriage, adultery and parenthood the novel portrayed. Funnily, I found that living in England has 'anglicized' my imagination. I kept visualizing Vronsky – the guards officer who abandons the army for a lover and a spot of painting – in brightly coloured corduroy trousers and suede chukka boots, like some Chelsea lizard.

2. Milos Tsernianski, *Migrations* (1978)

This is quite possibly the greatest Serbian novel, written in 1929. The story of two Isakovich brothers who escape Ottoman Serbia for Austria-Hungary in the eighteenth century, one to become an officer in the Austrian army, the other a wealthy merchant, may sound distant and obscure, but the way Tsernianski writes about love, sex, war, nation-hood, and exile grips one by the throat and does not let go. This tale of migration and longing for the safety of Russia and the North – is told in prose so beautiful that I still catch myself reciting the sections of it I have learned at school with a mixture of melancholy and awe.

3. Robert Dessaix, *Twilight of Love: Travels with Turgenev* (2004)

In his life and in his writings, the nineteenth-century Russian novel-ist Turgenev was a connoisseur of unusual passions. For forty years he remained devoted to the French opera singer Pauline Viardot. He accompanied her and her husband around Europe, often living next door to them or even in the same house, while his relationship with Pauline remained more or less chaste. I say 'more or less' because the archaeology of human relationships is an impossible science. We often don't know much about the passions of the people apparently closest to us; is it then possible to be certain about Viardot and Turgenev after more than a century had elapsed, when even the very substance of love might have changed? What I understand by 'I love you' might be very different from what Turgenev might have meant. Dessaix's exploration of this unusual affair defies generic boundaries. It is a detective story, a travelogue, a personal memoir, a piece of intellectual history and a fascinating examination of whatever love means.

4. Eva Hoffman, *Lost in Translation* (1989)

In their judgements on *Chernobyl Strawberries*, readers and reviewers often drew my attention to works which they considered in some way similar. Some comparisons were flattering (Robertson Davies, for example), others puzzling (Tom Sharpe). Eva Hoffman's name cropped up from time to time even while I was still writing the book. 'She is similar to you', a friend told me, 'and your histories are similar. You must read it'. Eva left Poland for Canada when she was twelve, went on to study at top American universities and produce a range of highly respected books: similarities are relative. I hate to admit this, but Eva's book had, for quite some time, languished on my reading pile enthusiastically purchased but as yet unopened, where she was in the company of some of the best writers of our time. I always buy at least three times as many titles as I can possibly read; a greed doubtless rooted in the reading hunger of my East European childhood. One of the first things I did after I submitted the manuscript of *Chernobyl Strawberries* to the publisher – now safe from what Harold Bloom calls 'the anxiety of influence' – was to read *Lost in Translation*. I enjoyed it so much that I instantly added it to my university course lists. Because this normally means that I have to reread the book again and again, such inclusion is more than a mere compliment.

5. Graham Swift, *The Light of Day* (2003)

I had noticed *The Light of Day* in the bookshops when it came out and read some good reviews, but decided that it was probably not my sort of book. The story of a private detective who follows an unfaithful husband around a relatively small patch of South West London, and develops a strange bond with his client, the jealous wife, seemed too understated for my taste. Now I wonder if my background (let's call it Continental) simply conditioned me to be attracted to books laced with more obvious literary fireworks? I heard Graham Swift read from *The Light of Day* last June. Something about the way he performed the text, in an amazing double-act of the writer and his character, alerted me to the possibility that there was nothing simple and very little that is parochial about this story. Anyway, I have now read it and changed my mind. It is absolutely my kind of story.

6. Rebecca West, *Black Lamb and Grey Falcon* (1942)

This is my favourite travel book. It is half-a-million words long and deals with a country that doesn't exist any more. I realise that many people might take a look at it and say: 'Well, it is about Yugoslavia, and it is broadly sympathetic towards the Serbs, so Vesna would say that, wouldn't she?'. I plead 'not guilty'. It is true, the fact that it was about Yugoslavia initially led me to it, but what West loved most about Yugoslavia are its southern and western parts, rather than the north-eastern area I came from. The historian A. J. P. Taylor called it a work of genius, and the American travel writer Robert Kaplan said it was the greatest travel book of the twentieth century. Rebecca West discovered Yugoslavia on the eve of the Second World War because – in the growing certainty of the apocalypse which was facing Europe – she wanted to write a book about a small country and its relationship with the great empires. Finland was an early, rejected choice. Written against the sound of bombs raining over London, this book is as much a memoir of one of the last century's most remarkable British women as it is an account of Yugoslavia.

7. Edmund Gosse, *Father and Son* (1907)

While I was undergoing treatment for cancer, *Father and Son* offered unexpected solace. First published anonymously in 1907, this book tells the story of Edmund Gosse's strange and solitary Victorian childhood. His parents were deeply religious members of the Plymouth Brethren. Gosse's mother, Emily, who died of breast cancer when Edmund was eight, authored a number of religious pamphlets. The account of Emily's cancer treatment in mid-nineteenth century London made my own treatment in early twenty-first century London seem luxurious, notwithstanding the spartan hospital wards and shared bathrooms, and all the problems familiar to any fellow user of our National Health Service. What Emily had, however, and I could not have, is an unwavering belief in God. I can certainly see the advantage of belief in such extreme situations, if not otherwise. I read her story as told by her son with enormous curiosity. It is a very unusual and very courageous book.

8. John Buchan, *Greenmantle* (1916)

'There is a dry wind blowing through the East, and the parched grasses wait the spark': the story of *Greenmantle*, which sweeps through London and Constantinople, via places such as Baghdad, Berlin and Belgrade, is my favourite adventure novel. I like Buchan's central character, Richard Hannay, the South African mining engineer and war hero, but his Sandy Arbuthnot is my favourite officer-and-gentleman: 'Tallish, with a lean, high-boned face and a pair of brown eyes like a pretty girl's... He rode through Yemen, which no white man ever did before... He's blood-brother to every kind of Albanian bandit. He used to take a hand in Turkish politics, and got a huge reputation...' *Greenmantle* is deadpan, a bit camp, full of imperial swagger, superbly plotted and absolutely irresistible.

9. George Eliot, *Middlemarch* (1871–2)

I hate to admit this, but although I might prefer a comparison to a broad range of femmes fatales of East European fiction, if anyone asked me to which literary character I think myself most similar, I would have to say that it was George Eliot's Dorothea Brooke. When I was younger I shared her idealism and her bookishness and I even had one or two crushes on highly unsuitable elderly Casaubons at the time when I still believed that it was possible to write the *Key to All Mythologies*. At twenty I used to think book-writing much more important, and even more sexy, than running a bank or a country.

10. C. D. Wright, *Steal Away: Selected and New Poems* (2002)

I discovered C. D. Wright's work while I was writing *Chernobyl Strawberries*. I felt a renewed thirst for poetry. I enjoyed those ten or twenty minute journeys elsewhere that the best poems offer and I didn't feel like engaging with stories or novels, perhaps because my own story preoccupied me so much at that time. A close friend recommended C.D. Wright, an Arkansas poet. Her poems are like words on fire, direct, often erotic, told in an unmistakably Southern voice. I've revisited this book so often that I now half-remember most of it. Strangely enough, the descriptions of Arkansas made me think of my own childhood. I remembered cycling furiously along narrow paths cut through maize fields, gripping the handlebars with fingers sticky and purple from picking wild mulberries. My sister and I spent sweltering evenings on our balcony, gossiping in the shelter of mosquito nets. We watched moths as big as eggs dive unsuccessfully towards the tiny holes. They flew towards the light, hitting the fine wire again and again. We were poor in almost everything else but rich in time.

11. Danilo Kis, *Garden, Ashes* (1965)

Kis's Jewish-Hungarian father died in Auschwitz. His own life was saved by the fact that his Montenegrin mother had him baptised to the Orthodox Christian faith in 1939, when he was four. In 1947 she took Danilo and his sister to Cetinje, the tiny former capital of the kingdom of Montenegro. Hidden in a nest of rocky mountain peaks, Cetinje is a picturesque town of Mediterranean stone houses incongruously mixed with the palaces and ornate embassies of the Great Powers, but Danilo's literary imagination remained deeply marked by the former Austro-Hungarian towns of his early childhood. From Cetinje, he went to Belgrade to study and then finally to France. He died in Paris in 1989, at the age of fifty-four. Although it employs a fictional form, *Garden, Ashes* is a journey around Danilo's father. It is a short, atmospheric and poignant book. I can't think of many others in which poetry and novel-writing come so close together.